THE PSYCHOLOGY OF LIFE

A GUIDE TO A LIFE OF MEANING AND PURPOSE

SUANTAK DEMKHOSEI VAIPHEI
FARIZA SAIDIN

"To My Loving Daughter Kimpahhawi Vaiphei"

My Love, My Joy, My Pride

Contents

Contents

FOREWORD

The Psychology of Life: A Guide to a Life of Meaning & Purpose is a comprehensive guide designed to help young people tackle the myriad challenges of modern life. This book begins by exploring the intense academic pressures, and mental health issues students face today, providing practical tips and strategies for effective studying and time management. It delves into life meaning and purpose challenges young people encounter, offering useful and valuable advice on finding meaning, and purpose and motivating them to achieve their goals and targets. Mental health is a crucial topic covered in this guide, featuring personal stories about coping with stress and depression, along with tips for managing these challenges and seeking help when needed.

The impact of social media on self-esteem and body image is another significant issue explored in this book. Through real-life experiences, it offers tips for healthy social media use to foster a positive self-image. Career indecision and exploration are addressed with stories and guidance on career planning, pursuing passions, and making informed career choices. Inspirational stories of resilience and growth emphasize the importance of learning from challenges and adopting a growth mindset. The book concludes by recapping key lessons and advice, encouraging and motivating readers to move forward with confidence. This book explores the challenges that youth experience, and provides context to better understand the factors related, to and contributing, to those issues. It captures the essence of the youth of its era and the timeless challenges of growing up.

Dr. Suantak Demkhosei Vaiphei

Preface

The book Psychology of Life: Guide to a Life of Meaning and Purpose can help you feel more confident and optimistic about life. Unlearning faulty programming through positive steps of life is the crux of the book. If you are a young learner, this book will orient your life. If you are a parent, it will help you to guide your children. If you are a teacher, this will be an aid to motivate your students. The titles inside are signboards serving as stop-points to reflect and enhance yourself to take steps for life's journey. This book explores the role of meaning, commitment, and creativity in finding purpose in life.

I hope that you enjoy the book, giving something worth making, and overcoming all the fear, procrastination, and self-sabotage that come along with it. It is fun and easy to read from a psychological perspective of how different people find purpose in the work they do. Since the topic of purpose is so subjective, the stories in this book are incredibly helpful. There isn't a right and wrong way to find purpose and happiness. There's only one way that works for you. "The Psychology of Life" extracts a framework from the theories to help you find your way into the thing that works for you.

Dr. Suantak Demkhosei Vaiphei

Acknowledgements

This book is the result of support from many good people. I want to express our appreciation and gratitude to all those who provided us with the opportunity to complete this work. I'm grateful to my parents (S. Hemkhai & Lhingkim Vaiphei) who planted the seed of knowledge in my mind and nurtured it wholeheartedly. Thank you, Mum and Dad. Without your unconditional support, this book never would have come to be.

I extend my deepest gratitude to my families and loved ones for their understanding and unwavering support throughout my challenging journey. Their encouragement was immensely motivating. I would not have been able to get my work done without the support and understanding of my wife (Chinhat Vaiphei) and daughter (Kimpahhawi Vaiphei), who provided a stimulating academic environment.

Furthermore, I want to acknowledge the contributions of my co-author, who has played a significant role in completing this book. I also express my heartfelt thanks to my peers and colleagues for their constructive feedback and wonderful collaboration, which enriched the intellectual discourse of this project work.

Prologue

"The mystery of human existence lies not in just staying alive, but in finding something to live for."
                    — Fyodor Dostoyevsky, The Brothers Karamazov.
Leaving a purposeful life involves emphasizing what genuinely matters to you based on your values and beliefs, followed by taking regular steps toward those priorities. Living with intention is profoundly individual; no one can direct your soul's calling. You will recognize that you are living intentionally when life appears genuine and satisfying, brimming with limitless prospects for development, expansion, and enthusiasm. If you've ever experienced this thought, find solace in knowing you're not by yourself. There is plenty of anecdotal proof that individuals are seeking methods to lead a more purpose-driven life. Leading a significant life and determining what holds significance are timeless inquiries (for instance, Marcus Aurelius contemplated this issue while he ruled as Emperor of Rome from 161 to 180 AD). The quest for meaning in life originates from two disciplines: philosophy and psychology. The philosophical inquiry seeks to comprehend the significance of life overall, along with our part in that significance. For this article, we will set aside the philosophical viewpoint on this matter. As psychologists, we are unable to add to this answer. Nonetheless, the second version of this question – how we derive meaning in life – is psychological and holds more significance for us.

Reker and Wong (1988) contend that the concept of meaningfulness is more effectively elucidated and comprehended through a three-dimensional framework that includes coherence, purpose, and an additional element: significance. Significance relates to the feeling that our existence holds meaning and that life possesses intrinsic value. Collectively, these three elements enhance a sense of significance. In certain studies, coherence, purpose, and significance have been redefined as cognitive and motivational processes. In particular, Heintzelman and King (2014) propose a framework consisting of three elements: goal orientation, significance, and life having meaning. Goal direction and mattering serve as motivational elements and are associated with purpose and importance, respectively. The third element – the sense that one's life has meaning – is a cognitive aspect, similar to significance. Together, these three elements – coherence, purpose, and significance – produce sensations of meaningfulness. Understanding that meaningfulness comes from three different areas, let's explore methods to uncover our meaning.

Discovering meaning is, at its core, a personal quest. What provides me with meaning may not provide you with meaning. Nevertheless, this doesn't imply that the methods employed to discover meaning will be ineffective. Viktor Frankl (1959) endorsed the idea that discovering purpose is a distinctive journey when he stated in Man's Search for Meaning: *"Man's search for meaning is the primary motivation in his life and not a "secondary rationalization" of instinctual drives. This meaning is unique and specific in that it must and can be fulfilled by him alone; only then does it achieve a significance that will satisfy his own will to meaning."* Building healthy relationships with other people and nurturing these connections are effective methods to foster a sense of purpose (Heintzelman & King, 2014). While social ties are significant, not every social relationship holds the same value. Ensure you concentrate on connections that give you a sense of 'belonging' (Lambert et al., 2013), where you feel aligned with the group members, and where there is a sense of group identity.

Motivation serves as a key factor influencing human behavior. It drives rivalry and ignites social interaction. The lack of it can result in mental disorders like depression. Motivation involves the drive to pursue meaning, purpose, and a fulfilling life. Intrinsic motivation arises solely from internal sources; it is not influenced by any expected reward, time limit, or external influence. For instance, individuals who are intrinsically driven to run participate because they enjoy the sensation of running itself, and it plays a significant role in their identity. External motivation may boost drive temporarily, but over time it can diminish or even have adverse effects. In contrast, intrinsic motivation is strong as it becomes part of one's identity and acts as a constant source of inspiration. Many individuals are driven by external rewards that originate from outside of us — for example: receiving a promotion, achieving high grades, posting on social media, and gaining validation from others.

When you experience feelings of being stuck or indifferent, "spend some time at the moment, whether it's by breathing, meditating, doing yoga, or journaling." "Being grounded in the present will enable you to take actions that can improve your mood and make you feel more like your true self." "If you require relaxation and self-care, pay attention to those signals and engage in beneficial activities to rejuvenate your body." This may involve activities such as exercise, spending time outdoors, meditation, a relaxing bath, or anything that represents self-care for you. Dividing tasks into smaller segments that progress toward the final objective can assist in organizing thoughts about the procedure. Concentrating on the specific tasks required to finish a project can assist in remaining present and focused. Acknowledge the small details by celebrating each task you finish - it can accumulate rapidly! Engaging in mindfulness can assist you in concentrating on and valuing each moment and the 'little' actions you take, like rising from bed or brushing your teeth in the morning. Every night, consider writing down three small victories you've accomplished that day, keeping in mind that any achievement, no matter how minor, is always worth celebrating. Embrace your present feelings, recognize the emotion, and seek support if necessary. Engaging in self-care and treating yourself kindly can be very beneficial when facing low motivation.

I

The Psychology of Living a Purposeful Life

"The purpose of life is not to be happy. It is to be useful, honourable, compassionate, and have it made some difference that you have lived and lived well."

— Ralph Waldo Emerson

Living a purposeful life involves giving priority to what is truly important to you based on your values and beliefs, and consistently taking steps towards those priorities. Living a meaningful life involves living by your beliefs and interests and experiencing happiness and satisfaction. Living a purposeful life involves finding satisfaction in aligning with your authentic self, making a positive impact on others, and always seeking personal growth and knowledge. It's about transitioning from just surviving to thriving completely. Leading a purposeful life is an ongoing process, not a set end goal. Living a purposeful life is guided by your internal compass - your fundamental values, passions, and morals. In contrast, an ordinary life may feel unexciting and without drive, but a purposeful life is fulfilling and impactful.

Why Should You Seek a Purposeful Life?

Having a sense of purpose boosts self-worth, inspires personal and professional development, and leads to greater happiness and fulfillment. It enables you to make a positive impact on the world and results in a more fulfilling and enriching life journey. Discovering oneself and understanding one's beliefs is the initial step to living a meaningful life. Self-reflection is necessary to comprehend your values, strengths, weaknesses, and passions. This includes examining yourself in the mirror and evaluating your behaviors, decisions, and reasons behind them. Once you know yourself, you can focus on becoming the person you want to become. Self-improvement involves recognizing imperfections, gaining wisdom from errors, and working towards self-growth. Keep in mind, that the aim is progress, not perfection.

Creating a list of your top priorities can help you identify your core values and guide your decisions and actions. Once you have identified your values, it is crucial to make sure your behavior aligns with them. It might mean standing up for your beliefs, choosing a profession that lets you make a difference, or investing in relationships that improve your health. The foundation of living a meaningful life is aligning your behavior with your beliefs. We live on purpose simply by walking out our values. We can accomplish this in various ways, whether they be significant or minor, throughout all seasons, regardless of external circumstances. This is within our power to manage. Living a purposeful life has several advantages:

- Improved emotional and physical well-being.
- Having a purpose in life could promote Happiness and better sleep.
- Increased productivity in the workplace.
- Encouraging positive thinking and confidence.
-

Satisfaction with life

- Stronger personal and interpersonal relationships.
- Enhanced physical/bodily capabilities in old age - Feeling that your actions have value is important for healthy ageing.
- Having a purpose in life reduces all-cause mortality and increases Life Longevity

What Gives Life Purpose?

Having a sense of purpose in life is a fundamental idea in positive psychology that is connected to general happiness. A recent study suggests that having a sense of purpose goes beyond mere motivation. It is a lasting characteristic. Northwestern University's Gabrielle Pfund (2023) suggests that there are a minimum of three distinct methods to assess a sense of purpose in life.

- **Brief Purpose Measure** (1.There is a direction in my life. 2. My plans for the future match my true interests and values.)
- **Purpose In Life Scale** (1.I live one day at a time and don't think about the future (reverse-scored). 2. My daily activities often seem trivial and unimportant to me (reverse-scored). 3. Some people wander through life, but I am not one of them.)
- **Life Engagement Test** (1.To me, the things I do are worthwhile. 2. I value my activities a lot. 3. I have lots of reasons for living.)

The importance of purpose is crucial, but how we interpret it may be even more significant. Our perception of life and our emotional state are greatly influenced by our perspective, demonstrating a dual relationship between our minds and bodies. While we may not have the ability to influence all events, we can tackle life directly by nurturing our self-awareness, self-compassion, and willingness to take imperfect actions. Here are a few psychological strategies for leading a meaningful life.

- **Set Goals:** Establish significant objectives/goals that provide you with a feeling of purpose and individuality.
- **Accept Discomfort:** Embrace and take responsibility for the discomfort you face in life, rather than attempting to evade it.
- **Practice Gratitude:** Make a conscious effort to acknowledge and appreciate the good things in your life - Donate Time, Money, or Talent.
- **Explore Your Interests:** Find out what you are passionate about by exploring your interests and discovering what activities bring you joy.
- **Use your character strengths:** Utilize your strengths to participate in activities that satisfy you.

Above all, be kind to yourself and surround yourself with Positive People. Choose to treat yourself with compassion rather than being overly critical or perfectionists. Set boundaries to establish a healthy divide between important and unimportant tasks. Discovering your purpose cannot be achieved quickly within a matter of days, weeks, or months. Achieving this goal may take a lifetime, so it's important to focus on one step at a time. Sometimes, you may discover that your goals evolve as time goes on. Taking time to assess whether your actions are in line with your goals is crucial. If not, you can choose to change your direction. Sometimes, the journey to finding your purpose can be filled with turns, divergences, and cues.

❧

References

1. Frankl, V. (1959). *Man's search for meaning.* Beacon Press.
2. Heintzelman, S. J., & King, L. A. (2014). Life is pretty meaningful. *American Psychologist, 69*(6), 561–574. https://doi.org/10.1037/a0035049

3. Pfund, G.N. (2023). Applying an Allportian trait perspective to sense of purpose. *Journal of Happiness Studies, 24,* 1625–1642. https://doi.org/10.1007/s10902-023-00644-4

• 5 •

II

Toward a New Definition of Mental Health

Many myths and misunderstandings exist regarding mental health. This can complicate the process for individuals with mental health issues to seek and obtain suitable assistance and exacerbate the stigma they encounter. They can also hinder the public's comprehension of mental health. Mental health includes our emotional, psychological, and social well-being. It affects how we think, feel, and act, and helps determine how we handle stress, relate to others, and make choices. Mental health is a term used to describe emotional, psychological, and social well-being. A person's mental health quality is often measured by how adaptively they can cope with everyday stressors. Mental health is important at every stage of life, from childhood and adolescence through adulthood. Good mental well-being entails the capacity to think, feel, and respond in the ways necessary and desired for living your life. However, during a time of poor mental health, you may discover that your usual patterns of thinking, feeling, or reacting become challenging, or even unmanageable, to handle. This can be just as distressing as a physical sickness, or potentially even more so.

Origin and New Definition of Mental Health

Before mental health, "mental hygiene" was a term used in the 19th and 20th centuries to refer to mental processes' impact on overall health. A major obstacle to integrating mental health initiatives into global health programs and primary healthcare services is the lack of consensus on a definition of mental health. There is little agreement on a general definition of 'mental health' and currently there is the widespread use of the term 'mental health' as a euphemism for 'mental illness.' *Mental health* can be defined as the absence of mental disease, or it can be defined as a state of being that also includes the biological, psychological, or social factors that contribute to an individual's mental state and ability to function within the environment. For example, the WHO includes realizing one's potential, the ability to cope with normal life stresses, and community contributions as core components of mental health. Other definitions extend beyond this to also include intellectual, emotional, and spiritual development, positive self-perception, feelings of self-worth and physical health, and intrapersonal harmony. Prevention strategies may aim to decrease the rates of mental illness, but promotion strategies aim at improving mental health. The possible scope of promotion initiatives depends on the definition of mental health.

In fact, regarding well-being as a key aspect of mental health is difficult to reconcile with the many challenging life situations in which well-being may even be unhealthy: most people would consider as mentally unhealthy an individual experiencing a state of well-being while killing several persons during a war action and would regard as healthy a person feeling desperate after being fired from his/her job in a situation in which occupational opportunities are scarce. People in good mental health are often sad, unwell, angry, or unhappy, and this is part of a fully lived life for a human being. Despite this, mental health has often been conceptualized as a purely positive effect, marked by feelings of happiness and a sense of mastery over the environment. Aware of the fact that differences across countries in values, cultures, and social backgrounds may hinder the achievement of a consensus on the concept of mental health, the study aimed at elaborating an inclusive definition, avoiding as much as possible restrictive and culture-bound statements. The concept that mental health is not merely the absence of mental illness was unanimously endorsed, while the equivalence between mental health and well-being/functioning was not, and a definition leaving room for a variety of emotional states and for "imperfect functioning" was drafted. The proposed definition is reported herewith:

"Mental health is a dynamic state of internal equilibrium which enables individuals to use their abilities in harmony with universal values of society. Basic cognitive and social skills; ability to recognize, express, and modulate one's own emotions, as well as empathize with others; flexibility and ability to cope with adverse life events and function in social roles; and harmonious relationship between body and mind represent important components of mental health which contribute, to varying degrees, to the state of internal equilibrium."

The concept of "dynamic state of internal equilibrium" is meant to reflect the fact that different life epochs require changes in the achieved equilibrium: adolescent crises, marriage, becoming a parent or retirement are good examples of life epochs requiring an active search for a new mental equilibrium. This concept also incorporates and acknowledges the reality that mentally healthy people may experience appropriate human emotions – including for example fear, anger, sadness, and grief – whilst at the same time possessing sufficient resilience to timeously restore the dynamic state of internal equilibrium.

Causes of Mental Health Issues

Mental health issues do not stem from a single source, but rather from a variety of factors that can increase the likelihood. While the precise origins of most mental disorders remain unclear, research is increasingly indicating that numerous such conditions stem from a blend of biological, psychological, and environmental influences. Numerous mental disorders tend to occur within families. However, that doesn't guarantee you will have one just because your mother or father did. Certain conditions engage circuits in your brain that are utilized in thinking, mood, and behavior. For example, there could be an excess or deficiency of certain brain chemicals known as neurotransmitters in those circuits. Brain injuries are also associated with certain mental disorders. Certain mental health disorders can be triggered or exacerbated by psychological trauma experienced during childhood or adolescence. Significant stressors, like a death or divorce, issues in family dynamics, unemployment, academic pressures, and substance misuse, can provoke or worsen certain mental disorders in some individuals.

However, not all individuals who experience those situations develop a mental illness. It's common to experience grief, anger, and various emotions after facing a significant setback in life. A mental disorder is distinct from that. In 2020, the number of individuals suffering from anxiety and depressive disorders increased notably due to the COVID-19 pandemic. Preliminary estimates indicate a rise of 26% and 28% for anxiety and major depressive disorders in merely one year. Although there are effective prevention and treatment options available, the majority of individuals with mental disorders lack access to adequate care. Numerous individuals also endure stigma, discrimination, and breaches of their human rights.

References

1. The American Psychiatric Association (2015). Understanding Mental Disorders. https://www.psychiatry.org/

UnderstandingMentalDisorders

2. WHO. 2008 Policies and practices for mental health in Europe—meeting the challenges. http://www.euro.who.int/__data/assets/pdf_file/0006/96450/E91732.pdf.

3. Vaiphei SD, Sisodia DS. Emerging issues and needs to focus on mental health and well-being in India: a qualitative analysis. Journal of Clinical Medicine of Kazakhstan. 2019;4(54):10-4. https://doi.org/10.23950/1812-2892-JCMK-00707

III

Learning For Change

Our country's higher education institutions are requested to fulfill significant responsibilities in establishing the ability for interactive collaboration and joint efforts for collective action to tackle intricate issues that are influencing the world we inhabit. A crucial aspect of building healthy communities such as education involves promoting fairness and diversity. The Oxford Dictionary describes learning as acquiring skill knowledge or expertise through studying, experiencing, or receiving instruction. The traditional concept of Teaching is a teacher-dominated affair. It is a process by which a teacher helps learners achieve knowledge, skill, and attitude. However, Pedagogue Paulo Freire, considered this concept oppressive, as it deprives the learning group of itself, especially in articulated education, where the teacher cannot play the role of judge, debater, or doctor. Freire argued that education is about conversations between learners and educators and this act of dialogue is called 'Conscientization'. The teacher's responsibility is to guide learners in defining, analysing, and designing solutions to problems. Conscientization and problematization should result in action and reflection that extend beyond the educational environment. Mahatma Gandhi always emphasized to educators the importance of nurturing inner motivations and using education to gain a deeper understanding of life. The teacher cannot rely solely on what he learned in the past for his entire life. One lamp must keep burning its flame to light another lamp. A teacher who teaches his topic and only repeats his lessons to students without engaging with his knowledge cannot stimulate their minds or inspire them. The realm of knowledge and skills constantly evolves and expands, so the quest for acquiring them is endless and nothing is set in stone.

Education is an active procedure that involves intentionality, organization, and purpose. It stimulates and evokes inactive energies and creative impulses. The main characteristic of the self is that it is a phenomenon that reflects upon itself. Reflexivity allows individuals to treat themselves as objects, or to contemplate themselves, have internal debates, assess themselves, and more. This quality of being human, rooted in the social aspect of language and the skill of taking on different roles, allows people to view themselves from another person's point of view and develop a self-concept. The chance to learn presents itself when the individual meets at the crossroads of their own life and their current environment. The acquisition of knowledge is a mixing of various procedures where the individual, with their physical and biological attributes as well as their cultural and mental characteristics, encounters a social scenario, which is then mentally, emotionally, or practically processed and absorbed into their personal history, ultimately leading to personal growth or change. The self is constantly shaped through interactions with important people in a person's life and different social environments. When the environment and social circle undergo significant changes, it may be necessary to reevaluate certain aspects of one's identity to adapt to the new world and societal expectations.

Theoretical Framework

George Vaideanu is the pioneer in discussing education for change as a new aspect of education. He has a deeper understanding of the goal of education for change, which is to ensure that humans remain the focal point of development. The goal of education is the individual, shaping to fulfill the needs of society. Man is both the doer and the recipient of the changes: "Everything is accomplished by man and for the good of man." The System for Learning and Developing Strategies and Skills (SLDSS) model emphasizes acting and empowering clients in social work, mental health, and human service settings to address individual needs and life goals. Jarvis's learning model is beneficial for organizing and understanding shared personal experience narratives. Jarvis categorizes nine forms of learning into three main groups: non-learning, non-reflective learning, and reflective learning. The model sees non-learning as harmony or assumption. The assumption is that we are in sync with our lifeworld and simply accept our world, personal experiences, and knowledge. When we are out of sync with our lifeworld, we feel disjuncture, also called cognitive dissonance in social psychology and disorientation in transformative learning. Internal disjuncture occurs when there is a lack of internal harmony within us. This is the moment when we frequently look for transformation in our lives. External disjuncture is viewed as an external factor that leads to learning, as something in our external environment prompts us to restore balance with our lifeworld.

Throughout our existence, we must give significance to our encounters. These experiences and interpretations shape our understanding of the world, representing the structures that guide our reactions and incorporating our morals, convictions, and presumptions that influence our actions. When deciding to scrutinize and update our existing beliefs and assumptions, we experience intellectual growth through changing our perspective. The transformative learning theory revolves around learning and changes that transform our lives and perceptions of ourselves, our environment, and the world. Existential transformation is questioning our old beliefs and experiences while considering new events or realizations and assigning new meanings to our lives and experiences. Life is centred around understanding how to exist in our environment. Discovering how to navigate a new environment, translating our fresh encounters into significance, and adapting to coexist in various worlds, we inevitably transform. This type of learning involves all aspects of a person and needs both time and space. Revising one's life circumstances and adapting to the resulting challenges requires a deep and varied process of learning at every level.

Despite what we are often taught in our youth, learning does not solely involve memorizing answers. It's more than just education and obtaining credentials. Learning is not assessed through exams, which only evaluate our grasp of theories, but is determined by evaluating its practical value through hands-on experience. Personal growth and development are the main focuses of individual learning. It helps boost self-confidence, problem-solving skills, effectiveness, performance, and overall experience utilization. Anticipation extends beyond foreseeing and selecting favorable trends while steering clear of disastrous ones. It also generates fresh options. Participation is more extensive; it necessitates the engagement of everyone in the process of transformation, from regular citizens to those in positions of authority. Participating allows one to engage in broader connections and perceive the interconnectedness of individuals within a larger entity. Problematization is considered the best approach for an education focused on creating change.

Despite some progress made in recent years, resistance to change often hinders transformation decisions' actual impact. Resistance to change is frequently encountered in innovation, primarily stemming from individuals' rigid perception of reality. It is beneficial to provide educational change processes, problem-solving models, and constant renewal to prevent ingrained habits or behaviors. Despite being contradictory, it is common for the individuals who should be advocating for change, such as teachers and trainers, to be the ones who resist it the most. Therefore, to make a change in education feasible, it is essential to influence them, their beliefs, and their mindset.

-Life is learning - Life is change - You live, you learn, you change -You change, you learn, you live.

&

References

1. Cranton, P. (2006). Understanding and promoting transformative learning: A guide to educators of adults (2nd Ed.). San Francisco, CA: Jossey-Bass.
2. Elizabeth Anne Erichsen (2011). Learning for Change. Journal of Transformative Education; 9(2):109-133.
3. Murtonen & Lehtinen (2020). Adult learners and theories of learning. https://www.researchgate.net/publication/346765351_Adult_learners_and_theories_of_learning.
4. Ona Anghel (2021). Education for Change. Review of Artistic Education; 22(1): 270-274

IV
How to Stay Focused While Studying

"Spoon feeding in the long run teaches us nothing but the shape of the spoon."

— E. M. Forster

Studying is not the same as reading, studying is difficult. Maintaining focus while studying is a challenge faced by both experienced Ph.D. students and young high school freshmen alike. Being distracted greatly affects your capability to focus. To concentrate on academic tasks, you may need to modify your studying routine, find a quiet setting free from distractions, try new approaches, or create a well-organized study timetable with frequent mental breaks. Continue experimenting with various techniques until you find what works best for you. Having the proper organization can make it easier to concentrate. Here are some simple study tips to help you stay focused.

- **Understanding Attention & Learning:** The field of Cognitive Psychology describes Attention as the process and mechanism of how individuals use sensory receptors to process information from their environment. Attention is a term used to explain how focused stimuli are processed more quickly and accurately than unfocused stimuli. It has a significant impact on our perception of our environment. Another crucial element of behavior is an individual's capacity to acquire knowledge. Learning is commonly divided into two fundamental types: explicit and implicit. Implicit learning occurs when individuals naturally and effortlessly acquire knowledge about the complex stimulus environment's underlying structure without actively engaging in conscious thought. Explicit learning involves a deliberate process in which the person creates and verifies hypotheses while seeking patterns.

Directing attention to increase the efficiency of processing and decrease attentional resources to unwanted or irrelevant inputs is fundamental to staying focused while studying. Applying a Behavioral approach to learning, which centres on the environmental influences (associations, reinforcements, and punishments) on the learning process, is also an essential factor for staying focused while studying.

- **Lev Vygotsky Techniques**: Vygotsky held the perspective that learning occurs actively within the framework of social engagement. He also thought that advanced cognitive abilities, like language and logic, are developed by engaging in culturally significant activities with other people. Maintaining concentration can be accomplished through utilizing a strategy that involves seeking guidance from someone with greater expertise to acquire fresh knowledge. The more knowledgeable educator dissects the information into smaller steps to aid the learner in comprehending and enhancing the study's appeal.
- **Constructivist Learning Techniques**: Constructivist methods emphasize that students learn best when they are actively involved in generating knowledge, instead of just passively receiving information. Utilizing constructivist methods such as assimilation and accommodation, individuals can dig deep into

a topic, research answers to their inquiries, and formulate their conclusions. Engaging in problem-solving activities and self-assessment through interactive self-reflection helps individuals understand their performance level and discover ways to enhance it.

- **Avoid Cramming**: Cramming is ineffective for long-term memory retention. However, reviewing and processing information makes you stay focused and makes learning effective. This approach enhances memory and understanding, helping you retain information better over time. It gives you a chance to review key details several times. Repetition is one of the best ways to improve your memory and stay focused.
- **Used Chunking**: Chunking is a method used to help short-term memory by breaking up large amounts of information into smaller, more manageable chunks to enhance concentration and understanding.
- **Use Mnemonic Rhymes**: Rhymes, alliteration, and jokes are not only effective methods to recall routine information but also make learning enjoyable and help to stay focused.
- **Visualize Concepts**: Creating mental imagery of the things or lessons you are studying will make learning easier and increase concentration.
- **Relate New Information to Things You Already Know**: Establishing relationships between new ideas and previously existing memories can dramatically increase the likelihood of staying focused and help concentrate on recently learned information.
- **Mix It Up**: Interleaved practice is a method where various skills are mixed while studying. It is crucial to ensure that the skills being blended in interleaved practice are interconnected.
- **Figure Out What Works for You**: Applying metacognitive ability (ability to effectively evaluate one's approach to learning and level of attainment) is found to be an effective method of learning in academia.

Taking university-level courses may prove to be difficult since students are exposed to different teaching and learning techniques that are unfamiliar to them. Due to the diversity of courses/subjects, students may feel overwhelmed by the vast amount of information they need to grasp. Utilizing your preferred methods and employing concept mapping are both effective ways to liven up your studying routine and boost your focus. Kolb's concept of active/reflective and abstract/concrete in the Converged and Diverged approach may also be a valuable strategy for improving learning and focus. Concentrate on developing your comprehension of a subject instead of simply regurgitating someone else's ideas to make learning more enjoyable and engaging. Making sure to incorporate retrieval practice into your study routine is equally important. Finally, take sound sleep, keep yourself hydrated, and give yourself a break.

ॐ

Learn more on how to stay focused while studying from:

1. https://oxfordsummercourses.com/articles/how-to-stay-focused-while-studying
2. https://www.etbi.ie/wp-content/uploads/2022/08/NCGE-PP-Helping-Concentrate-Study-PDF-EN.pdf?x33691
3. https://www.kstate.edu/counseling/services/resources/self_help/improvingconcentration.html
4. https://www.youtube.com/watch?v=dguuBM09PKM

V

Pendemic: Youth the Most Vulnerable Group

Pandemic COVID-19 and post-Covid have changed the course of life as people spend around 90% of their time indoors and even more in some cases. The lockdown period gives rise to new challenges for the general population to focus on holistic well-being. Well-being is no longer an option; it is the strategic driver for talent advancement. The World Health Organization (WHO) defines *health* as "a state of complete physical, mental, and social well-being and not merely the absence of disease or infirmity." However, the general understanding of health/well-being in India is still confined to physical health. The absence of a holistic understanding of health and well-being in our society could be mainly due to a lack of knowledge/education and proper awareness. The minimal availability of mental health workers and services provided could also be another factor. Cultural beliefs and social stigma hugely affected the general population by minimizing their understanding of health and well-being, mainly confining it to physical health, while ignoring the other existing aspects.

The outbreaks of COVID-19 not only affect people's physical health, it also hugely affect people's psychological, social, and neuroscientific dimensions. This pandemic has had huge negative impacts on individual mental health like acute stress, post-traumatic stress disorder, anxiety, depression, irritability, insomnia, and decreased learning attention among the college and school goings. Apart from the general population the students/youngsters have a special attachment to the social group based on their relationships, contacts, and college/university activities. However, the pandemic has changed the life of these youngsters drastically, due to the lockdown and university/college restrictions. This could be the underlying reason why youngsters are visible as the most vulnerable group, who are likely to have anxiety and depression almost double that of the general population. The youngsters are also visibly experiencing negative psychological symptoms like substance abuse, eating disorders, and loss of self-control. These radical behavior changes amplified the burden on the mental health of this vulnerable population, which demands special consideration. Uncertainty regarding technological concerns, academic success, future careers, and job loss are among the other concerns. Moreover, even before the covid-era youngsters experienced a higher prevalence level of anxiety, mood disorder, lack of self-esteem, substance abuse, psychosomatic problems, suicidality, and other mental disharmonies. These are the underlying reasons why the youngsters in our society need additional care services to help them with their ongoing physical and mental health issues, which are the repercussions of the pandemic.

It is to be noted that psychological symptoms like PTSD, OCD, Acute Stress Reaction, Major Depression, Adjustment, and anxiety disorders do not fully cover all the dimensions caused by this pandemic. The increasing rate of suicidal ideation and suicide among youth and those who lost their jobs due to the pandemic is another current challenge. Suicidal thoughts and other self-harm activities can also be triggered by isolation and untreated psychological problems during the lockdown period. For youngsters, school/college routines are an important coping mechanism concerning their mental health issues. On the other hand, the closing of schools/colleges can relapse their mental health symptoms and for some, it is like losing the anchor of their life. Society needs to realize that living with mental disharmony and emotional suffering are symptoms to be treated like other physical symptoms. The mental health issue is a consistent problem without an ideal solution, which requires proper acknowledgment and diagnosis. The minimal availability of trained mental health professionals and the current social stigma are visible as the common barriers to people seeking mental health support in the state. Some of the self-help tips to overcome mental health issues are:

1. Avoid or have little exposure to media coverage to reduce anxiety and develop an attitude of positive thinking.
2. Maintain healthy relationships and get in touch with friends and loved ones.
3. Share your fear/anxiety with friends and loved ones and get adequate sleep.
4. Exercise regularly and develop different relaxation techniques like meditation and so on.
5. Enhance self-awareness and be able to recognize the warning signs of mental health problems (like unusual problems functioning, or dramatic changes in sleep and appetite)
6. Learn how to keep your stress levels in check (almost anything that affects your daily life) and remember that some stress can be helpful. However, too much stress may make you ill.
7. Eat a brain-healthy diet to support strong mental health and avoid fast food, alcohol/drugs, caffeine, and foods with high levels of chemical preservatives or hormones.
8. Find purpose and meaning in life (engaging in work that provides meaning to yourself and others)

9. Value yourself (treat yourself with kindness and respect, and avoid self-criticism)
10. Be extra kind to yourself and find ways of expressing kindness, patience, and compassion through volunteering, etc.
11. Spirituality could be another coping mechanism (staying connected with the God/transcendent being)
12. Get help when you need it (mental health problems such as anxiety or depression can lead to worsening symptoms)

And remember, seeking help in times of need is a sign of strength and not weakness. It is your mental health that influences the way you think, feel, and behave, and affects your inner ability to cope with the stressors. When talking about healthy mental health, it is not just the absence of psychological or mental health problems, but rather the ability to deal with them with positive characteristics. There is an urgent need to understand the mental perspectives of this pandemic among the youth and children. The need of the hour is to take up possible measures to cope with the pandemic and its effective management. It is also equally important to acknowledge the mental health concerns of those with COVID-19, close contacts, healthcare professionals, and the general population.

VI

The Psychological Benefits of Sports

There is always a misconception among Indian parents that sports affect children's academic careers, resulting in keeping away their children from playing any sports activities during their school and college life. However, sports are an activity that yields significant outcomes for individuals of all ages. Several pieces of research evidence suggest that sports participation is positively associated with more healthy behaviors, improved school performance, improved subjective health, and increased well-being in young people. It also develops teamwork skills, self-confidence, resiliency, moral character, and other personal strengths, especially among the youth and children. Playing sports like boxing, swimming, and other physical activities helps one's brain work better in terms of memory and cognition, which also performs better in academic domains. Additionally, discipline and perseverance—two qualities associated with athletic success—are crucial for improved psychological health and academic achievement.

Benefits of Playing Sports: Character Building Traits

- Self-confidence and self-esteem – self-concept and peer acceptance among the sports person have a strong positive effect on self-esteem, most significantly physical self-esteem.
- Manage Emotions, Social skills, Patience and Perseverance
- Accept defeat - Sports educate youngsters at a young age that success is not guaranteed.
- Teamwork and Respect Authority - Following a set of rules, accepting decisions, and taking direction is a big part of playing any sport, which usually gives rise to teamwork and respect.
- Leadership Skills – leading a team often entails developing abilities such as communicating with teammates, handling team emotions, taking the lead, and so on.
- Lifelong Habits - Sports teaches children to take care of their bodies through proper food choices, which usually form a lifelong character.

Psychological and Physiological Benefits

- Beats stress, anxiety, and depression - Physical activity stimulates the production of endorphins - the hormones that relieve stress and pain. Participating in any sports activity will boost mood by diverting the individual mindset from any bothersome thoughts.
- Improves focus and concentration – The foundation of all sports is focus and being focused; participating in sports often helps people become more focused and focused both on and off the field.
- Self-discipline - A key component of any athletic endeavor, self-discipline is a valuable quality that aids in personal growth and the accomplishment of life's goals.

- Reduced risk of obesity and Increased cardiovascular fitness
- Regulates blood pressure and Improves energy levels
- Reduces blood sugar levels and Strengthens lungs
- Improves coordination and balance - Engaging in any activity necessitates a certain level of hand-eye and foot-eye coordination that ultimately moulded an individual.
- Helps prevent cancer - fitness activities lower the incidence of cancer, especially cancers of the colon, prostate, uterine, and breast.
- Reduces chronic muscular tension and improves sleep

Sports have positive effects on physical and emotional health, regardless of age. Children who play sports from a young age typically form lifelong habits and lifestyles that benefit them. It even helps people extend their physical health and improves their mental health. It is not advisable, nevertheless, to see participating in sports as a physically demanding activity that you should undertake for your health. To make sports more fulfilling and pleasurable, it is necessary to make them a lifetime pastime. In addition to the advantages to one's physical and psycho-emotional well-being, sports careers can lead to success in other spheres of life.

References

1. Thapos. Benefits of Sports. https://sportsplus.blog/coaching-parenting/benefits-of-sports/
2. Meenakshi Nagdeve. Benefits of Playing Sports. https://www.organicfacts.net/health-benefits/other/health-benefits-of-playing-sports.html

VII

Understanding Drug/ Substance Abuse Disorder

Drug abuse or substance abuse refers to the use of certain chemicals to create pleasurable effects on the brain. When you're able to change your unhealthy habits of drug abuse to feel good, ease stress, or avoid reality, you are addicted to it. Drug/substance addiction is a disease that affects your brain and behaviour. When you're addicted to drugs, you can't resist the urge to use them, no matter how much harm the drugs may cause. Despite being aware of these harmful outcomes, many people who use drugs continue to take them, which is the nature of addiction

What happens to the brain when a person takes drugs?

Almost all drugs affect the human brain's "reward circuit," causing euphoria as well as flooding it with the chemical messenger dopamine. A properly functioning reward system motivates a person to repeat behaviours needed to thrive, such as eating and spending time with loved ones. Surges of dopamine in the reward circuit cause the reinforcement of pleasurable but unhealthy behaviour's like taking drugs, leading people to repeat the behaviour again and again.

Thus, in continuation, the brain adapts by reducing the ability of cells in the reward circuit to respond to it. This reduces the high that the person feels compared to the high they felt when first taking the drug—an effect known as tolerance. They might take more of the drug to try and achieve the same high. These brain adaptations often lead to the person becoming less and less able to derive pleasure from other things they once enjoyed, like food, sex, or social activities.

Long-term use also causes changes in other brain chemical systems and circuits, affecting functions such as learning, Judgment, Decision-making, Stress, Memory, and Behaviour (*National Institute on Drug Abuse; National Institutes of Health; U.S. Department of Health and Human Services, 2018*).

Cause of Drug/Substance Abuse

People from all walks of life can experience problems with the usage of drugs, regardless of age, race, background, or the reason they started using drugs in the first place. It is usually psychoactive drugs that people use for various reasons which may include:

- Curiosity and peer pressure, especially among school children and young adults
- The use of prescription drugs that were originally intended to target pain relief may have turned into recreational use and become addictive
- Chemicals may be used as part of religious practices or rituals
- Recreational purposes
- As a means of obtaining creative inspiration
- To ease problems such as stress, anxiety, or depression.

Risk factors for drug addiction

While anyone can develop problems from using drugs, vulnerability to substance addiction differs from person to person. While your genes, mental health, family, and social environment all play a role, risk factors that increase your vulnerability include:

- Family history of addiction, and Environmental influences
- Abuse, neglect, or other traumatic experiences
- Psychological factors/Mental disorders such as depression and anxiety
- Early use of drugs, and Low health literacy
- Method of administration—smoking or injecting a drug may increase its addictive potential

Overcoming Drugs/Substance Addiction

Most people who engage in addictive behaviours and go on to develop an actual addiction find that overcoming it is more challenging than they expected. Like other chronic diseases such as heart disease or asthma, treatment for drug addiction usually isn't a cure. However, addiction can be managed successfully. Treatment enables people to counteract addiction's disruptive effects on their brains and behaviors and regain control of their lives. Depending on your lifestyle and needs, you may choose one of the following types of programs:

- **Residential** – Residential treatment facilities are typically a good option for someone with a severe problem. In these programs, patients get round-the-clock care, counseling, and treatment. If you go this route, it's important to follow up with an outpatient or group therapy as you re-acclimatize daily life.

- **Day treatment** – If you want to maintain your residence but still need extensive care, day treatment may be a good option. This way, you'd receive care all day and then go home at night.
- **Outpatient** – Outpatient programs are designed to help recovering addicts maintain their everyday lives, including work and school responsibilities. Outpatient programs work well for people who have a substance abuse problem that isn't a full-blown addiction or people who have just completed residential rehab.
- **Sober living** – In a sober living home, you'll live with recovering addicts in a safe, supportive environment. You'll get to maintain a job and focus on sobriety (*2011 - 2021 SkillsYouNeed.com*).

For many people struggling with addiction, the toughest step toward recovery is to recognize that you have a problem and decide to make a change. Recovery requires time, motivation, and support, but by committing to change, you can overcome your addiction and regain control of your life. Here are some of the tips to overcome drug addiction:

- Remind yourself of the reasons you want to change.
- Surround yourself with supportive people Tell friends and family that you're committing to recovery, and ask for their support
- Set specific, measurable goals, such as a start date or limits on your drug use.
- Find new hobbies, Do regular exercise and Eat well
- Seek professional help

Addiction is a long-lasting yet manageable health issue. Many individuals, often unknowingly, continue to discuss addiction in stigmatizing manners—implying they use terms that can depict someone with a substance use disorder (SUD) negatively or shamefully, potentially deterring them from pursuing treatment. By making straightforward adjustments in language, harmful stigma and negativity associated with SUD can be mitigated or eliminated. Continue reading to discover more about the nature of stigma, its impact on individuals with SUD, and ways you can contribute to making a difference. No single test exists to identify substance use disorder. Instead, healthcare professionals depend on a comprehensive assessment of your medical background and habits related to substance use. They might request drug tests to determine the quantity and variety of substances present in your body simultaneously. They might also assess reports from prescription drug monitoring programs (a database of distributed controlled substances). The initial stage of treating substance use disorder is managing withdrawal. This is the point at which you cease using the substance, permitting it to exit your body. Based on the intensity, a healthcare professional might prescribe drugs to alleviate the impact of withdrawal symptoms, which can be challenging both physically and psychologically. Substance use disorder treatment is very personalized. You may require various forms of treatment at various stages throughout your recovery. Various forms of treatment environments are available, including inpatient and outpatient facilities, along with short-term care and long-term therapeutic communities.

"What is addiction? It is a sign, a signal, a symptom of distress. It is a language that tells us about a plight that must be understood."

– Alice Miller on the true meaning of drug addiction recovery

For information about understanding drug use and addiction, visit:

www.nida.nih.gov/publications/drugs-brains-behavior-science-addiction/drug-abuse-addiction

https://nida.nih.gov/publications/drugfacts/understanding-drug-use-addiction

VIII

The Psychology of Fight or Flight Response

"While the fight-flight-freeze response causes physiological reactions, it's triggered by a psychological fear" - Nunez, K.

This article is to help students organize their ideas on psychology conceptually. I expect most of the information I teach my students will not be remembered. However, I believe that they will remember the importance of psychology in understanding behavior, and cognition processes, as our understanding of psychology is rooted in scientific studies.

The instinct to 'fight or flight' has existed since ancient times and remains crucial for coping with stress and threats in our environment. The fight-or-flight response is a quick response to danger that produces physical changes in the body's nervous system and hormone levels, preparing an individual or animal to either face the threat or run away from it. American physiologist Walter Cannon coined the term after observing the body's rapid and unconscious response to obtain resources in threatening situations. He also referred to it as the acute stress response. A stress response is how your body responds to a threat, whether it is perceived as real, imagined, or anticipated. Assisting in swift responses to stressful or life-threatening situations is a typical aspect of life. Your response will be determined by the stimulus and past traumatic events. Walter Cannon observed that when an animal encounters a predator, their bodies produce epinephrine and adrenaline hormones, triggering the fight or flight response. This mechanism operated automatically and helped the animal protect itself during dangerous situations by preparing the body for either fleeing or fighting.

The stress response happens when the requirements of the surroundings surpass our perceived capacity to handle them. An individual's stress levels are impacted by their emotions towards a situation and their coping skills. From a biological perspective, these hormones play a critical role in starting a speedy and thorough response. A decrease in blood pressure, discomfort, bodily injury, rapid emotional distress, or decreased blood sugar may all result in this response. It might also result from a sensory disorder like misophonia, where there is an extremely negative response to certain sounds or their triggers. The fight-or-flight response involves increased heart rate, anxiety, sweating, shaking, and higher blood sugar levels from glycogen breakdown. In individuals and animals under chronic stress, simultaneous brain and hormone reactions like increases in corticotropin and cortisol secretion occur alongside other stress responses, leading to prolonged activation of the fight-or-flight response.

During the fight-or-flight response, your body shifts its attention to prioritizing tasks, suspending anything not crucial for immediate survival. This means that processes such as digestion, reproduction growth hormone release, and tissue healing are all momentarily stopped. Rather, your body is directing all its energy towards the most crucial priorities and functions. The stress response can be activated abruptly, but the time it takes to relax and return to your normal state varies between people and is affected by the cause. Normally, it generally takes around 20 to 30 minutes for your body to return to its usual state and unwind. Duke clarifies that our fight-or-flight response was designed to help us survive in dangerous situations. Today, it could be said that there are less risks to our existence. The fight-or-flight response is an essential reaction required by everyone, but it is meant for real stress and danger. If you observe your body reacting to daily stress with a fight-or-flight response regularly, you can focus on gaining back a feeling of control. The fight-or-flight response has a specific function, but it should not be activated by everyday stressors like traffic, emails, or bills. If this occurs, it is crucial to identify when the response is activated and go back to your initial condition.

The fight-or-flight response should only be triggered when it is needed or beneficial. The sympathetic nervous system activates the body's response, while the parasympathetic nervous system restores the body to a state of calm. Controlling your stress response is essential for your overall well-being. When you find yourself getting overly stressed about something that isn't a real danger, it is crucial to consider the broader perspective. If stress is negatively affecting your daily life, seeking help from a healthcare professional could be beneficial. Therapeutic interventions, prescription drugs, and stress-coping strategies can assist in achieving a more equilibrium state. With time and regular practice, individuals can improve their abilities to regulate their stress reactions and avoid any detrimental impacts. It is always vital to seek assistance when needed. If you are concerned about your mental, and physical health, or both, make sure to prioritize yourself.

References

1. Cleveland Clinic (2024). What Is the Fight, Flight, Freeze or Fawn Response?   https://health.clevelandclinic.org/what-happens-to-your-body-during-the-fight-or-flight-response.

2. Nunez, K. (2020). Fight, flight, or freeze: How we respond to threats. Healthline. https://www.healthline.com/health/mental-health/fight-flight-freeze#overactive-response.

3. Adam Augustyn (Oct. 2024). fight-or-flight response. https://www.britannica.com/science/fight-or-flight-response.

IX

Suicide Awareness: Re-Thinking Suicide Attitude

"It is okay to feel lost and unsure. Your journey is unique, and every step forward is a sign of strength." — *Unknown*

Suicide is death caused by self-inflicted injury with the intent to die. It's common among all age groups and affects many people. Suicide doesn't always have clear warning signs. It can happen suddenly, without any indication that something is wrong. Suicide doesn't always have clear warning signs. It can happen suddenly, without any indication that something is wrong. Suicide is a significant public health issue that necessitates a response from public health. We have reached a point where we cannot overlook suicide and must not turn a blind eye to it, since it continues to be one of the primary causes of death globally. By employing timely, evidence-supported, and frequently affordable measures, suicides can be averted. It is a complicated human behavior influenced by several interacting factors. As per the latest WHO report, annually, more individuals succumb to suicide than to HIV, malaria, breast cancer, or war and homicide combined.

It is estimated that over 700,000 individuals take their own lives each year. The issue of suicide prevention has not been sufficiently tackled because of insufficient awareness regarding suicide as a significant public health concern and the cultural taboos surrounding open discussions about it in numerous societies. Stigma, especially related to mental illnesses and suicide, causes many individuals contemplating suicide or who have attempted it to refrain from seeking assistance, resulting in them not receiving the necessary support. As of now, only a limited number of nations have made suicide prevention a part of their health priorities, with just 38 countries indicating they possess a national suicide prevention strategy. Increasing community awareness and dismantling the stigma is crucial for nations to advance in suicide prevention initiatives. Worldwide, the suicide rate is declining; in India, it is increasing. Currently, India is experiencing a continuous rise in the suicide death rate, which is calculated as the number of suicide fatalities per year per 100,000 individuals. Crude suicide rate (not age-adjusted) and the following are the Suicide rates in India 2000-202, as per the World Bank report:

- India's suicide rate for 2019 was **12.70**, a **0.79% increase** from 2018.
- India's suicide rate for 2018 was **12.60**, a **5% increase** from 2017.
- India's suicide rate for 2017 was **12.00**, a **0.83% decline** from 2016.
- India's suicide rate for 2016 was **12.10**, a **1.63% decline** from 2015.

Studies indicate that the majority of individuals who plan to commit suicide make some effort to communicate their intentions to others before taking action. These "warning signs" include individual actions and verbal and non-verbal expressions. Mental and emotional disorders like depression and bipolar disorder are frequently associated with suicidal thoughts. The likelihood of suicide might be highest as the individual's depression starts to improve. Numerous factors contribute to suicidal thoughts. Suicidal thoughts usually stem from challenging and depressive life circumstances (For instance: feeling unable to manage when confronted with what appears to be an insurmountable life issue). At this moment, lacking hope for the future might lead you to believe that suicide is a remedy incorrectly. You might go through a form of tunnel vision, where during a crisis, you think that suicide is the sole escape. Conversely, there could also be a hereditary connection to suicide. Individuals who commit suicide or experience suicidal thoughts or behaviors are more prone to having a family background of suicide. While suicide is a heartbreaking occurrence, it can be averted by recognizing the warning signs and knowing how to seek immediate assistance and professional care. Doing so may save a life — your own or someone else's. Some of the suicide underlying risk factors are:

- Previous suicide attempt(s)
- A history of suicide in the family and Substance misuse
- Mood disorders (depression, bipolar disorder)
- Access to lethal means (e.g., keeping firearms in the home)
- Losses and other events (for example, the breakup of a relationship or a death, academic failures, legal difficulties, financial difficulties, bullying)
- History of trauma or abuse (Family violence, including physical or sexual abuse)
- Chronic physical illness, including chronic pain
- Being exposed to others' suicidal behaviour, such as that of family members, peers, etc.

In some cases, a recent stressor, abrupt disastrous incident, or setback can cause individuals to feel hopeless, unable to envision a solution and become a "tipping point" leading to suicide. A relationship issue was the primary factor leading to suicide, followed by a crisis experienced in the previous or next two weeks and troubling substance use.

Prevention and Diagnosis

The good news is that suicide is preventable and treatable. Preventing suicide requires strategies at all levels of society. The following are some of the strategies:

- Identify and Assist Persons at Risk (Examples of activities in this strategy include gatekeeper training, suicide screening, and teaching <u>warning signs</u>)
- Ensure Access to Effective Mental Health and Suicide Care and Treatment **(Safety Planning,Collaborative Care, Cognitive Behavioural Therapy, Dialectical Behaviour Therapy).**
- Respond Effectively to Individuals in Crisis (Teach coping and problem-solving skills through social-emotional learning programs)
- Provide for Immediate and Long-Term Postvention (Lessen harms and prevent future risk)
- Reduce Access to Means of Suicide (Create protective environments access to lethal means among persons at risk of suicide)
- Promote Social Connectedness and Support (Promote Connectedness-Peer norm programs-Community engagement activities

Most people can be helped in getting through their moment of crisis if they have someone who will spend time with them, listen, take them seriously, and help them talk about their thoughts and feelings. Suicide is linked to mental disorders, particularly depression and alcohol use disorders, and the strongest risk factor for suicide is a previous suicide attempt. Some individuals at risk for suicide might benefit from medication. Most importantly, no single approach can do it all. "When you're thinking about suicide prevention, you've got to think at many levels all at once." However, many of them may have been dealing with mental health challenges that had not been diagnosed or known to those around them.

❧

Learn more about Suicide and Suicide Prevention from:

1. https://www.cdc.gov/suicide/prevention/index.html
2. https://www.sprc.org/effective-prevention/comprehensive-approach
3. https://www.psychiatry.org/patients-families/suicide-prevention

X

Workplace Trauma Is Real

"Trauma is personal. It does not disappear if it is not validated. When it is ignored or invalidated the silent screams continue internally heard only by the one held captive. When someone enters the pain and hears the screams, healing can begin."
– Danielle Bernock

"What doesn't kill you makes you stronger; Except for workplace hazards, if they don't kill you, they can leave you with a life long disability."

Work has the potential to bring about growth and achievement, but it can also result in stress and trauma. Workplace trauma, also known as post-traumatic stress disorder (PTSD), refers to the mental or emotional distress employees endure while working. Work-related trauma or post-traumatic stress disorder is not listed in the DSM-5 but is gaining recognition for its importance. Work-related trauma can originate from a single traumatic incident or develop over time due to chronic stress and anxiety.

A person experiences trauma when they interpret a certain situation or multiple situations as being risky or endangering their life. While unique to individuals, trauma usually has lasting negative effects that impede the capacity to succeed in different areas of life, including mental, physical, social, emotional, and spiritual health.

There are no set rules on what experiences qualify as traumatic. It all depends on how you react to them. Different individuals have varying perceptions of what constitutes as traumatic. Others cannot comprehend your emotions towards your personal experiences or decide if they are distressing for you. You might experience similar situations as someone else but have differing responses or outcomes that could have lasting effects. Work-related trauma can lead to significant levels of anxiety, depression, and burnout in workers, which can subsequently lead to increased absenteeism, conflicts, decline in job satisfaction, and decreased productivity.

The most challenging part is that work-related trauma is frequently overlooked. Work trauma impacts not only employees' professional lives. This intrusion into their personal lives can cause a series of negative effects: straining their relationships, reducing their self-esteem, hindering their hobbies, and ultimately decreasing their overall well-being. Some of the factors contributing to workplace trauma are:

- Job Insecurity: Constant fear and stress of job loss or inability to advance in a career
- Bullying & Harassment: Verbal or physical abuse from colleagues and those in leadership, resulting in mental and emotional distress
- Exposure to Violence: Witnessing acts of violence or crime in the workplace
- Unfair Treatment like feeling discriminated against, ignored, or disregarded due to unfair policies or practices
- A toxic work environment and culture
- Excessive amounts of workplace stress
- Inadequate Support Systems

The Importance of Early Detection

Detecting trauma at an early stage can stop more psychological harm and promote a more nurturing work atmosphere. Employees who sense understanding and backing are more inclined to recuperate and resume productivity. Detecting and providing assistance early on can greatly impact their recovery and overall harmony in the workplace. Identifying early signs of symptoms is essential for preventing workplace trauma. Employees can take proactive steps to address potential issues before they escalate by recognizing the warning signs. Early symptoms may differ based on the kind of work, but some typical examples include Behavioral symptoms like increased sick days, aggression, reduced creativity, lower job performance, relationship problems, mood swings, irritability, and isolation; Physical symptoms such as stress, fatigue, headaches, changes in appetite, lethargy, anxiety, and panic attacks; Emotional symptoms like irritability, emotional outbursts, mood swings, paranoia, moodiness, and negative thoughts; Mental symptoms like feeling numb, difficulty sleeping, trouble concentrating, inability to stick to a routine, constant pressure to overwork, and relationship issues.

Organizations must prioritize mental health support in the workplace, emphasizing trauma-informed care and aid. Employers can take steps to reduce the worst impacts and assist their employees by actively striving to create a work environment that can withstand trauma.

Overcoming workplace trauma

Hierarchies in the professional environment can facilitate the occurrence of abuse. Employees are at risk due to a lack of victim protection, fear of reprisal, and potential harm to their livelihood. As we typically associate "abusive relationships" with our personal or family life, it can be challenging to identify them in a work setting. However, identifying this experience can be crucial to the healing process. Whether it occurs at home, work, or in the world, trauma is never your fault. You should receive assistance to recover. Here are some initiatives you can do on your own to overcome workplace trauma and experience the healing process:

- **Identify the Source:** Identifying the origin of the trauma is the initial step to address workplace trauma. Recognizing the source of trauma enables you to tackle the problem head-on and strive for a resolution to alleviate the stressors.
- **Don't Self-blame:** One common trauma response is self-blaming. Mostly, individuals who experience workplace trauma are not to blame for their mistreatment. Consider any regrets and wishes you may have about your past job as valuable lessons. Lessons to improve decision-making in your future job.
- **Give Yourself Time to Grieve:** This step is crucial for the healing process. Avoid suppressing your feelings or pressuring yourself to move on. Allow yourself to experience the pain, rage, and sorrow that accompany mourning. Keep in mind that your emotions are legitimate.
- **Reach Out to Your Support System:** Express your emotions with family, friends, or a therapist can be beneficial during challenging times. Opening may be challenging, but it is crucial to embrace vulnerability.
- **Know When to seek help:** If your distress is impacting your relationships, work, or daily life, you may have acute stress disorder or post-traumatic stress disorder (PTSD), but treatment for traumatic stress is not necessary for everyone.
- **Finding closure:** Achieving a sense of closure is crucial for maintaining good mental health. Without resolution, the mind tends to replay past events, seeking a different path that could have led to a more favorable result.
- **Set Boundaries:** It is crucial to establish boundaries on work hours and maintain clear distinctions between work and personal life. This enables you to unplug from work during your

time, allowing you to relax and re-energize.

- **Prioritize self-care:** Make sure to eat healthy food, exercise regularly, and have a restful sleep. And try to find alternative ways to manage stress, like engaging in art, music, meditation, relaxation, and enjoying the outdoors.
- **Self-regulate your nervous system:** Regardless of how upset, nervous, or overwhelmed you may be, it's crucial to understand that you can regulate your arousal system and soothe yourself. When you feel disoriented, confused, or upset, engaging in mindful breathing can quickly help you relax. Just take 60 breaths, paying attention to each exhale. Permit yourself to experience your emotions as they arise. Recognize your emotions related to the trauma as they surface and embrace them.

Toxic workplaces are harming the health and mental well-being of many workers. In recent years, more people have spoken out about these dangers inspiring hope that we might finally be able to make a difference for those who suffer from workplace trauma every day. The impact of workplace trauma can affect an employee's mental health, job performance, and overall quality of life. Traumatized individuals may experience symptoms such as anxiety, depression, flashbacks, nightmares, difficulty concentrating, and decreased motivation. Addressing trauma in the workplace is not only a moral imperative but a strategic necessity. By acknowledging the impact of workplace trauma and providing resources to promote healing and resilience, you can create a workplace where employees feel valued, safe, and empowered to thrive despite any challenges they may face.

The supreme lesson of any education should be to think for yourself and to be yourself; absent this attainment, education creates dangerous, stupefying conformity.

Bryant H. McGill

ജ

Learn more about Workplace trauma and how to overcome it from:

1. https://www.theguardian.com/commentisfree/2022/sep/21/workplace-trauma-can-affect-anyone-in-any-occupation-how-can-we-deal-with-it
2. https://pmc.ncbi.nlm.nih.gov/articles/PMC7123879/
3. https://www.bbc.com/worklife/article/20210415-why-long-term-workplace-trauma-is-a-real-phenomenon

XI
Why Do We Conform?

Conformity is the jailer of freedom and the enemy of growth. ... The opposite of courage is not cowardice, it is conformity.

Conformity bias is when individuals tend to act based on the behavior of others instead of relying on their own judgment. In today's digital age, conformity bias quietly influences user behavior, shaping decisions without conscious awareness. Users often follow the crowd, swayed by social proof rather than individual judgment. Conformity bias also referred to as social conformity, is a psychological phenomenon where individuals tend to go along with the group and agree with the majority, even if it may not be the optimal decision. This has the potential to influence our decision-making and constrain our capacity to think freely or generate innovative thoughts. The impact of social conformity bias in society is so powerful that human psychology and behavior cannot be fully understood without taking it into account. Conformity bias in social psychology is when individuals alter their behaviors, beliefs, or attitudes to match those of others.

What Causes Conformity Bias?

Knowing when we conform has various practical advantages in daily life, depending on your goals: it can aid in comprehending your own actions and predicting how others will act in various situations. Truly, the conformity bias can lead individuals to blindly mimic the group instead of relying on their ethical discernment. At times, we adhere to the group's norms to prevent appearing silly. This inclination can be especially powerful when we are uncertain about how to behave or when the expectations are unclear. Even though conformity is frequently criticized, it is not always a harmful influence. Conformity, when at its peak, provides a feeling of fitting in and being part of a group, as well as promoting individuals to follow ethical norms. At its most severe, it can reveal a person's most negative tendencies and even lead to the justification and execution of massive atrocities.

Typically, individuals conform due to their identification with a particular group. In practice, an individual must follow the norms and rules of the group to be fully embraced as a member. Individuals acquire social abilities at a young age by watching and imitating the actions of those around them. As people age, the societal expectations to adhere to group standards intensify. Experienced group members can employ different methods to influence newcomers to adhere, such as praising, criticizing, bullying, or demonstrating "appropriate" behavior.

A moderate level of conformity can result in greater social cohesion, at both individual and societal scales. Individuals adhere to social norms for different motivations, including both advantageous and disadvantageous factors. People conform for two main reasons: Informational Conformity and Normative Conformity. Individuals tend to conform to information when they lack knowledge or experience. They might also alter their actions to prevent appearing foolish or wrong. Individuals may conform to social norms to prevent being punished, mocked, or isolated for not blending in with the group. They might also adjust their behavior to gain approval or liking from other group members. There are numerous reasons why individuals conform to the group. Two of the main motivations are to gain knowledge and prevent being denied.

Types of Conformity

There are multiple types of conformity, including compliance, identification, internalization, normative conformity, and informational conformity. Kelman (1958) distinguished between three different types of conformity:

- **Compliance:** A public change in behavior, motivated by the desire to be accepted or avoid disapproval. A person may outwardly agree with the group, but privately hold a different opinion
- **Identification:** A deeper type of conformity than compliance, where a person changes their behavior to fit in with a social role. For example, a person might change their behavior to fit in with what is expected of them in a new role
- **Internalization:** A person changes both their public and private beliefs and behaviors. A person accepts the beliefs and behaviors of the group and believes they are correct
- **Normative conformity:** A change in behavior or belief due to the desire to be liked and accepted. Peer pressure is an example of normative conformity
- **Informational conformity:** A change in behavior or belief due to the desire to be correct. A person may look to the group for information, especially if they lack knowledge

Challenges in differentiating compliance from internalisation arise because it is difficult to assess public compliance versus private acceptance. For instance, an individual may concur with the group and subsequently adopt that viewpoint as their own. Compliance represents the least substantial form of conformity since it entails only surface-level and superficial alterations, ending when an individual is not within the group.

Factors That Influence Conformity

Multiple factors are linked to heightened conformity, such as larger group size, consensus, strong group cohesion, and perceived greater status of the group. Additional factors related to conformity include culture, gender, age, and the significance of stimuli. The reaction to conformity pressures differs based on various factors.

- While the most intelligent group members are less likely to conform, authoritarian personalities are more likely to do so:
- Where the membership of a group maintains both sexes, conformity levels are higher than in single-sex groups.
- Other variables that relate to increasing conformity are the size of the majority in favor, the ambiguity of the situation, agreement among most other members, and the open and decentralized nature of the group" communication systems.

Allen (1965) proposed that in addition to the issue of private and public approval, ten situational factors affect a person's reaction to group conformity pressures; some of these are:

- The level of commitment to the group
- The level of attractiveness of the group
- Status in the group
- The degree of interdependence within the group

Asch (1951) identified two main factors that affected conformity: the size of the group and the consensus within the group. The initial factor, group size, was shown by modifying Asch's original experiment to change the number of confederates. They discovered that raising the number of confederates from two to three resulted in an increase in conformity from 13.6% to 31.8%. However, no additional increases were observed, leading Asch to conclude that group size influences behavior only up to a certain limit. The second factor, group consensus, was shown by adding a confederate who was directed to provide the accurate answer together with the participant. The addition of this extra confederate reduced the error rate of participants from 35% to approximately 5.5%. In summary, Asch (1951) illustrated the influence of conformity within groups, noting that the primary factors impacting this conformity are group size and unanimity; nonetheless, group size influences conformity only up to a certain limit.

ॐ

References and Further Reading

1. Sherif, M. (1935). A study of some social factors in perception. Archives of Psychology, 27(187)
2. Robert B. Cialdini and Noah J. Goldstein (2004). SOCIAL INFLUENCE: Compliance and Conformity. Annu. Rev. Psychol. 55: 591–621. doi: 10.1146/annurev.psych.55.090902.142015
3. Quinn A, Schlenker BR (2002). Can accountability produce independence? Goals as determinants of the impact of accountability on conformity. Personal. Soc. Psychol. Bull. 28: 472–83.
4. Dalal, A. K. and Misra, G. (2010). The core and context of Indian psychology. Psychology and Developing Societies, 22(1): 121 – 155.

XII

What Makes Introverts Better Leaders?

Introverted leaders often display remarkable resilience in the face of challenges.

- The Introverted Leader

Extroverts have traits such as excellent public speaking skills and confidence, which enable them to be successful leaders, while introverts exhibit characteristics that render them empathetic managers who lead their teams to success. Introverts are people who typically appreciate peaceful alone time. They are often viewed as more introverted and sometimes shy compared to their extroverted counterparts. Due to their reserved natures, introverts might be perceived as unfit for positions of leadership. Nonetheless, recent studies have shown that introverted individuals can be more effective leaders than extroverted ones in specific circumstances. It's valuable to revisit the belief that extroverts make better leaders than introverts. Introverts and extroverts alike have the same opportunities for effective leadership. Optimal outcomes occur when every personality matches the requirements of their team.

What Makes Introverts Better Leaders

Leaders are frequently characterized using terms associated with extroversion: sociable, friendly, assertive, and energetic. However, frequently, the most effective leaders are introverts who have a subtle strength. Several factors contribute to introverts excelling as leaders, including their exceptional listening skills, thoughtful analysis, and greater empathy compared to extroverts.

- Introverted individuals tend to be more thoughtful when listening and are skilled at verifying comprehension. They prefer individual conversations rather than large group gatherings.
- Introverted individuals tend to analyze information thoroughly and deliberately before reaching conclusions. This can aid them in resolving issues with greater efficiency.
- Introverted individuals tend to be more understanding and exhibit traits related to emotional intelligence. They are also more inclined to pay attention to their behavior towards others.
- Introverts tend to be better leaders in dynamic, unpredictable environments because they are more effective in those situations. They are more open to feedback and can lead vocal teams more effectively.
- Promote A Positive Work Atmosphere: Introverts remain serene and foster a supportive ambiance. Workers appreciate having them as their leaders and trust that they will assist them during difficult situations.
- Introverts are typically reflective and tend to build deep connections.

While introverts can be effective leaders, they often do not progress to leadership positions in organizations that rely on traditional promotion and selection methods. Nonetheless, introverts are increasingly recognized for their importance in various contexts, including workplace environments. To foster increased diversity and inclusivity in their teams, businesses need to acknowledge and value the unique abilities of introverted leaders. By taking this action, a conducive and efficient work environment can be established to foster the development and success of each team member. Introverted leaders usually exhibit lower reactivity compared to extroverted leaders. They can stay calm and collected when facing pressure, enabling them to make improved decisions in stressful circumstances. Engaging in active listening with a positive mindset allows for collaborative and quicker problem-solving, unlike when approaching issues with confrontational or negative attitudes. Effective leadership can be characterized by positive settings where individuals are provided a voice that receives attention at the highest levels.

Quality of Self-Awareness

Certainly, extroverted leaders possess significant advantages. Nonetheless, they often have a way of dominating the spotlight and steering conversations. In a fast-moving, uncertain environment, introverted individuals tend to be more successful leaders—especially when employees take initiative, suggesting ways to enhance the organization. This kind of behavior can cause extroverted leaders to feel insecure. Conversely, introverted leaders often pay closer attention and demonstrate a higher openness to ideas, which enhances their effectiveness with outspoken teams. Numerous introverted leaders are inherently reflective and conscious of themselves. They spend time contemplating their choices and actions to guide from a more assured standpoint. Self-reflection aids introverted leaders in recognizing aspects that require enhancement. This self-reflection and consciousness may also result in being more sensitive to the emotions of those around you. Introverts often display greater empathy and compassion. As leaders, expressing empathy towards your team members is crucial, particularly during challenging periods such as when the pandemic struck.

Outgoing leaders often excel in overseeing unassertive workers. Inactive employees prefer a more straightforward method. At the same time, introverts flourish when leading proactive team members who have many suggestions for enhancements. The initial step for any aspiring introverted leader is to embrace their identity. Extroverts might be sociable and more assertive in the corporate environment, yet introverts contribute their distinct worth to the mix. Introverts possess the skills of assessing, analyzing, evaluating, and making careful decisions. Only by embracing their true strengths and supporting their choices with confidence can introverts rise to be exceptional leaders.

Learn more about introverted leadership from:

1. https://www.forbes.com/sites/karadennison/2024/02/14/why-the-future-of-leadership-will-look-to-introverts/
2. https://www.greatplacetowork.ca/en/articles/5-reasons-why-introverts-make-great-leaders
3. Grant, Adam M, Francesca Gino, and David A Hofmann. 'The Hidden Advantages of Quiet Bosses.' https://www.researchgate.net/publication/49712301_The_hidden_advantages_of_quiet_bosses

XIII

How to Set Goals with Youth

"You are never too old to set another goal or to dream a new dream." – C.S. Lewis

"A goal is a dream with a deadline." – Napoleon Hill

Numerous young people are missing the environments, activities, and milestones that provide organization in their lives. Urging them to establish goals can provide a framework that helps maintain their motivation and orientation toward the future. Establishing goals can assist young individuals in concentrating on their aspirations, maintaining motivation, and enhancing self-assurance. Goals provide us with a target to aim for, a reason to stay inspired, and with some fortune and considerable effort – something to cheer about. Acquiring the ability to establish goals is an essential skill for youth. Ultimately, it's difficult to reach a location without being aware of the destination you are aiming for. Aiming for goals assists teenagers in concentrating on the path toward their desired accomplishments, enabling them to create plans, manage their time and resources effectively, and recognize areas where they might require assistance.

Why is Goal Setting Useful for Young People?

Objectives aid in defining achievement. Individuals usually uphold their expectations rather than exceed them. Therefore, expectations or objectives ought to be difficult, but still attainable for an individual or a group. Objectives establish shared tasks and procedures for a team or individuals. With these, a group understands its tasks and can collaborate on achieving the objectives. Establishing goals requires time. At first, the members need to be familiarized with the process, acquire essential skills, execute procedures, and document assessments. Establishing organizational goals can be challenging when seeking objectives that all members support and will actively strive for. Many young individuals experience moments of uncertainty about how to reach their objectives, or even what those objectives ought to be. Establishing goals can assist young individuals in obtaining a sense of purpose, drive, and concentration. Establishing objectives enables young people to turn their thoughts into action. These abilities will benefit them personally, academically, and professionally. Understanding how to establish goals offers numerous advantages, including:

- Achieving the desired result (the ultimate goal of any goal!)
- Increasing self-confidence throughout the process
- Understanding and developing their work ethic
- Learning what works best to motivate them
- Building their perseverance when things don't go as planned
- Learning when to ask for help or support

Locke & Latham's Goal-Setting Theory

Locke (and later, in collaboration with Latham) initially released his innovative goal-setting theory in 1968. This study fundamentally altered the belief that establishing easy and broad goals enhances motivation and morale. For instance, "achieve high marks." Locke & Latham emphasized the significance of goals that are specific, measurable, and challenging. Aim for the stars, but not just any star; aim for that specific star over there. The five key principles of effective goal setting suggested by Locke & Latham are:

- **Clarity:** The goal needs to be straightforward, clear, and obvious to even outsiders.
- **Challenge:** Easy goals don't provide enough motivation to work hard. Design a challenging goal, but one that is still attainable. It's a fine balance!
- **Commitment:** Are you (and anyone else involved in achieving the goal) convinced that achieving this goal is important?
- **Feedback:** An effective goal is a goal in which you can assess your progress along the way, give feedback, and change course if need be.
- **Task complexity:** Highly complex goals can be overwhelming, often goals within goals within goals. Your goal should be manageable, without too many things going on within it.

The Big Leagues - SMART Goals

SMART is an acronym that describes some of the key elements to consider when setting goals. SMART stands for:

- **Specific** - It is easier to track progress when goals are specific. For example, the goal "I will be more active" is admirable but it is broad and hard to measure. A specific form of this goal could be "I will walk the dog for an hour, at least three times per week."
- **Measurable** - Encourage a goal that can be measured. How often will they do a particular activity? How much time will they spend on a daily, weekly or monthly basis to achieve their goal?
- **Achievable** - Goals that are too hard can discourage your teenager. Help your child set goals that will be challenging but

not unreasonable.

- **Realistic** - Encourage them to consider what kinds of goals are realistic given their personal circumstances.
- **Timely** - Time frames help provide a sense of structure and help your child know how they are going reaching their goal.

When establishing a goal, clearly define what you aim to achieve. Consider this as the guiding principle for your objective. Which metrics will you utilize to assess if you achieve the goal? This renders a goal more concrete as it offers a method to assess advancement. If the project will require a few months to finish, establish some milestones by identifying tasks to achieve. Milestones consist of a sequence of steps that, when combined, lead to the achievement of your primary objective. This emphasizes the significance of a goal to you and the actions you can take to achieve it, which may involve acquiring new skills and altering your mindset. The purpose is to encourage motivation, not to bring about discouragement. Anyone can establish goals, but without realistic timing, it's likely you won't achieve them. It's essential to set a target date for deliverables. Inquire about precise deadlines for the goal and what can be achieved during that timeframe. If the objective will take three months to accomplish, it's beneficial to outline what should be reached at the midpoint of the process. Imposing time limits also generates a feeling of urgency.

Benefits Of Goal Setting

The benefits of goal setting are real and significant. Goal setting applies both to you as an individual and to a group that sets goals.

- Improves your self-image (or the self-image of the group).
- Makes you aware of your strengths, which can be used to overcome obstacles and provide solutions to problems. (The same is true for the group.)

- Makes you aware of your weaknesses so you can begin to improve them and make them into your strengths.
- Gives you a sense of past victories and provides a stimulus for present successes.
- Helps you visualize. Plan actions to achieve the goals you set and then carry them out.
- Gives you a track to run on so you can see where you must go.
- Forces you to set priorities. Priorities establish the direction of your pursuits.
- Defines reality and separates it from wishful thinking.
- Makes you responsible for your own life. Makes your group responsible for its success or failure.
- Serves as a criterion to sharpen decision-making

ॐ

References

1. Bandura, A. (1986). Social foundations of thought and action. Upper Saddle River, NJ: Prentice Hall.
2. Locke, E. A., & Latham, G. P. (2002). Building a practically useful theory of goal setting and task motivation. American Psychologist, 57(9), 705-717.
3. Button, S., Mathieu, J., & Zajac, D. (1995). Goal orientation in organizational behavior research. Organizational Behavior and Human Decision Processes, 67, 26-48.

XIV
The Science of Mindfulness

"Empty your mind, be formless, shapeless—like water. Now you put water into a cup, it becomes the cup, you put water into a bottle, it becomes the bottle, you put it in a teapot, it becomes the teapot. Now water can flow or it can crash. Be water, my friend."

– Bruce Lee

Mindfulness is the extraordinary practice of mastering and regaining one's completeness, which has been linked to extensive theoretical and empirical studies demonstrating its influence on psychological well-being. Mindfulness-based interventions aim to enhance mindfulness by promoting awareness of one's current experiences with a perspective of equanimity and acceptance. Mindfulness is a mental characteristic, a condition of fostering awareness via mindfulness meditation and mental processes. In general terms, mindfulness is defined as "the non-judgmental awareness of the continuous flow of internal and external stimuli as they occur." Mindfulness, the capacity to cultivate deliberate non-judgmental awareness, originated in the Indian subcontinent around 2500 years ago. Nonetheless, mindfulness approaches in scientific research and therapeutic methods for prevalent psychological stress, anxiety, and depression started only in the 1970s. While mindfulness components significantly aid in alleviating clinical symptoms for improved life functioning, their application regarding positive human functioning remains unclear.

How Does Mindfulness Affect Health and Well-Being?

Mindfulness techniques can enhance health and well-being by assisting individuals in coping with stress, improving sleep, and promoting relaxation. Mindfulness can assist individuals in managing severe illness, anxiety, depression, and pain.

- Decrease Anxiety and Depression after meditation training.

- Improvement of the Immune System after meditation training.
- Meditation training might safeguard your brain against deterioration caused by aging and stress.
- After undergoing meditation training, mental clarity and focus are enhanced.
- After meditation training, you might experience less wandering of the mind.
- Meditation training may enhance your heart health.
- Mental health treatment is improved through meditation training.
- Meditation training might help slow cellular aging.
- Meditation training may enhance self-confidence and leadership skills.
- Meditation practice can enhance your mood.
- Meditation training might enhance sleep quality.

Research indicates that concentrating on the present may positively affect health and wellness. Mindfulness-based therapies have been demonstrated to diminish anxiety and depression. There is also proof that mindfulness can reduce blood pressure and enhance sleep quality. It might also assist individuals in managing pain. "According to Zev Schuman-Olivier of Harvard University, mindfulness meditation appears to enhance quality of life and lessen mental health symptoms for various chronic illnesses." Various fields and activities can enhance mindfulness, including yoga, tai chi, and qigong; however, the majority of research has concentrated on mindfulness cultivated through mindfulness meditation—self-regulatory practices aimed at training attention and awareness to achieve better voluntary control over mental processes, ultimately promoting overall mental health and development, as well as specific skills like calmness, clarity, and concentration (Walsh & Shapiro, 2006).

Types Meditation

Mindfulness can be engaged in through different approaches, each offering its distinct focus and advantages.

- **Focused Attention Meditation:** Concentrated attention meditation involves directing your focus on one specific object, thought, sound, or image. It highlights eliminating distractions from your mind and concentrating your focus on the selected point of attention.
- **Open Monitoring Meditation:** In open monitoring meditation, rather than concentrating on one object, you stay mindful of every facet of your experience as it unfolds. This form of mindfulness meditation includes watching your thoughts and emotions as they occur, without evaluating or engaging with them.
- **Body Scan Meditation:** Body scan meditation is a form of mindfulness practice that focuses on noticing various areas of your body in a progressive order. By mentally examining yourself, you increase awareness of each part of your body, observing any discomfort, tension, or pain you may be experiencing.

- **Loving-Kindness Meditation:** Commonly referred to as Metta meditation, this technique consists of sending positive thoughts to both you and others. It focuses on cultivating feelings of compassion and love, employing repeated phrases or intentions that assist you in concentrating on a sense of loving-kindness.

Mindfulness meditation is a flexible and easy-to-access practice that can be tailored to fit anyone's lifestyle or requirements. Regardless of whether you are managing stress, pursuing mental clarity, or trying to enhance your overall wellness, mindfulness provides a route to increased tranquillity and satisfaction. By comprehending the various forms of mindfulness meditation, applying successful techniques, and recognizing the significant advantages, you can start on a path toward a more mindful, balanced lifestyle. Keep in mind that the essential aspect of mindfulness is regular practice. The greater the integration of mindfulness into your life, the more benefits you'll experience. So inhale deeply, concentrate on the now, and allow the transformative effects of mindfulness meditation to improve your life.

How to Practice Mindfulness: 5 Mindfulness Exercises

Engaging in mindfulness activities can assist in reshaping your brain, shift your focus from distracting and negative thoughts, and help you connect with your environment while offering more organization to your thinking. Mindfulness meditation affects brain activity as well, facilitating a transition from the default mode network (which handles mind-wandering and self-referential thoughts) to the task-positive network (linked with present-moment awareness and concentrated attention). This change fosters enhanced mental clarity and the capacity to respond thoughtfully instead of reacting instinctively to life's difficulties.

- **Focus on your breathing:** Close your eyes and feel each breath as you inhale and exhale. If your thoughts wander, take note of them as objectively as you can, and bring them back to your breathing.

1. **Experience your environment:** Direct all of your senses—touch, sound, sight, smell, and taste—to your immediate surroundings.
2. **Live in the moment:** Find joy in the simple pleasures and the present activity you're engaging in.
3. **Take a walk:** Maintain awareness of your senses and the movements that keep your balance.
4. **Do a body scan:** Lie on your back with your legs extended and arms at your sides, palms facing up. Direct your focus to each part of your body in sequence, moving from toe to head or head to toe. Take note of any sensations, emotions, or thoughts associated with each part of your body.

The most encouraging aspect of these exercises is that you can perform them at any time and location, and they don't have to consume a large portion of your day. Just five minutes can be sufficient to gain some advantages if you establish it as a habit. Certain structured activities, like sitting meditation or body scan, are enhanced by a calm setting without distractions. Therefore, based on your location, you might choose a different workout. It's important to highlight that numerous studies indicate that practicing mindfulness meditation outdoors offers additional benefits.

Anxiety, stress, and depression are frequently intensified by concerns, anxieties, or reflections regarding the past or future. The advantage of increased present-moment awareness is that it enables you to concentrate more intensely on the now, which can change your viewpoint from worrying about the future or past to the moment you're experiencing. Regularly practising mindfulness will enable you to fully utilize this skill even when you're not meditating. By doing this, you will find that when you encounter difficulties, you can shift your attention to the present moment more effortlessly than if you weren't engaged in mindfulness meditation.

It is crucial to keep in mind that mindfulness is a practice that necessitates dedication and consistency to achieve enduring advantages. Like how physical activity fortifies the body, meditation serves as a mental workout that sharpens the mind. Consistency and patience are essential as the brain slowly adjusts and reorganizes itself over time. Whether you aim for stress relief, improved concentration, or emotional strength, the research indicates that mindfulness meditation can be an effective method to tap into your brain's capabilities and change your life. Why not spend a few minutes each day sitting, breathing, and experiencing the life-changing advantages of mindfulness for yourself?

ॐ

References

1. Allen, J.G., Romate, J. & Rajkumar, E. Mindfulness-based positive psychology interventions: a systematic review. BMC Psychol, 2021; 9, 116. https://doi.org/10.1186/s40359-021-00618-2
2. Goleman D, Davidson RJ (2017). Altered traits: science reveals how meditation changes your mind, brain, and body. New York, NY: Avery.
3. Michael Sayers W, et al., (2015). The emerging neurobiology of mindfulness and emotion processing. Springer EBooks; p. 9–22. https://doi.org/10.1007/978-1-4939-2263-5_2

XV

Social Media Addiction and mental Health

"*Social media is addictive precisely because it gives us something which the real world lacks: it gives us immediacy, direction, a sense of clarity and value as an individual.*"

— *David Amerland*

The impact of social media dependency on youth has become an increasingly important issue. Numerous mental health experts are concerned that kids and adolescents are especially vulnerable to becoming addicted to social media. This concern arises from how social media platforms promote endless scrolling, impulsive actions, and a craving for immediate satisfaction. For kids and teenagers, whose brains are still maturing, social media poses the risk of reshaping young minds to rely on immediate gratification and compulsive habits. Although it's difficult to determine which social media platform is the most habit-forming, the statistics indicate which sites have the highest screen usage. YouTube and Facebook are the most popular online platforms, with Twitter, Pinterest, LinkedIn, and Instagram trailing closely.

How Common Is Social Media Addiction?

The addiction to social media is a recent occurrence, but it has increasingly gained prevalence in recent years. A recent study suggests that a psychologist estimates nearly 10% of individuals will fulfill the criteria for some form of social media addiction. Social media is habit-forming due to its design. Every one of these social media platforms is structured to adjust their algorithms to ensure maximum user engagement continually. Grasping the influence of social media on our mental health and general well-being is essential for you and those close to you. For young people, browsing Instagram, Facebook, Reels, and various social media platforms is a typical part of our daily habits. In 2023, it was estimated that there were 4.9 billion social media users globally. On average, individuals dedicate 145 minutes daily to social media. Social media can adversely affect our overall health by intensifying anxiety, depression, isolation, and FOMO (fear of missing out). These problems are pervasive among teenagers and young adults.

Social media is permanent and will keep developing and becoming increasingly intrusive. Social media possesses a self-reinforcing quality. Utilizing it triggers the brain's reward center by releasing dopamine, a "feel-good substance" associated with enjoyable activities like sex, food, and social engagement. The platforms are created to be compulsive and are linked to anxiety, depression, and various physical issues. "The concept of a possible future benefit maintains the utilization of the machines. *"The same applies to social media platforms. It is unknown how many likes a photo will receive, who will 'like' it, and when those likes will occur. The unpredictable results and the chance of achieving a favorable result can maintain users' interest in the websites."*

Social media can serve as a strong means of connection, yet it may also contribute to heightened feelings of anxiety and depression—especially in teenagers. Today's kids and teenagers are unaware of life without digital technology, yet the digital landscape was not designed with the healthy mental growth of children in consideration. We require a strategy to assist children in both online and offline environments that accommodates each child's unique situation while striving to enhance the safety and wellness of their digital spaces. If you find yourself dedicating too much time to social media and experiencing emotions like sadness, dissatisfaction, frustration, or loneliness affecting your life, it could be a good moment to reassess your online practices and seek a more balanced approach.

How Does Social Media Affect Mental Health?

The compulsive quality of social media stimulates the brain's reward system through the release of dopamine. This is a "feel-good substance" associated with enjoyable experiences. When we share something, our friends and family have the option to "like" it, providing us with a dopamine surge. Nonetheless, when we fail to receive that support or validation, it can affect our self-esteem and feelings of worth. Social media is frequently referred to as a "highlight reel," showcasing the finest moments of a user's life. Nonetheless, viewing other people's highlight reels can heighten our feelings of discontent with our everyday lives. This may affect self-worth, provoke anxiety, and increase our desire to engage with social media. FOMO may drive individuals to frequently monitor social media to ensure they stay informed about current events.

- The application of 'Filters' on numerous social media platforms can be amusing, yet the ease with which one can modify their appearance and conceal flaws can lead to deceptive perceptions. Frequent exposure to modified images can make you feel insecure and dissatisfied with your appearance.
- Many individuals experience heightened feelings of FOMO due to social media usage. Looking at your friends and family on social media might give you the impression that they're enjoying life more or having a better time than you are.

- Cyberbullying occurs when an individual persistently and deliberately torments, abuses, or mocks another person using an electronic device. It can significantly affect self-worth and psychological well-being. Social media sites can be hotbeds for cyberbullying and disseminating harmful rumors, falsehoods, and mistreatment that can result in enduring emotional damage.

A research project conducted at the University of Pennsylvania discovered that extensive use of Facebook, Snapchat, and Instagram enhances feelings of loneliness instead of alleviating them. In contrast, the research revealed that decreasing social media use can decrease feelings of loneliness and isolation, enhancing your general well-being. People require in-person interaction for good mental health. Nothing alleviates stress and enhances your mood quicker or more efficiently than direct eye contact with someone who truly cares for you.

A Multi-Faceted Approach to Addressing the Issue

Nonetheless, tackling the intricate link between social media and mental health necessitates a comprehensive strategy that extends beyond the measures taken by social media companies. From a legal standpoint, this might encompass governmental regulation and personal legal measures. Policymakers might contemplate enforcing more rigorous regulations and standards for social media platforms, such as mandating that they prioritize user health and mental well-being above engagement and profit. This might involve requiring frequent mental health impact evaluations, offering resources for mental health assistance, and enforcing more stringent content moderation policies to limit the dissemination of harmful and toxic material.

Educational institutions also hold an essential role in fostering digital literacy and responsible social media behavior among students. Educational institutions ought to integrate digital literacy training into their programs and instruct students on how to use social media constructively and positively. Parents and caregivers should also participate in this process by establishing suitable limits and exhibiting responsible social media behavior, as parental oversight of media use positively influences various academic, social, and physical results for children (Gentile, et al., 2014). Increasing awareness through campaigns is crucial for addressing social media addiction, especially in young people. Education is essential for these initiatives as it enables young people to understand the dangers and impacts of overusing social media. Programs aimed at increasing awareness can help teens understand how social media might affect their relationships, mental well-being, and academic success. Awareness initiatives might include presentations in schools, workshops, and online tools that encourage teenagers to discuss their use of social media platforms. By promoting open discussions about personal challenges and experiences, such initiatives can reduce the stigma surrounding the prevalent problem of social media addiction while fostering a culture that supports transformation.

Mental health practitioners need to adjust to the evolving tech environment and include social media understanding in their therapeutic strategies. The NIMH highlights the significance of educating people on sustaining a positive relationship with social media, which involves establishing usage limits, participating in offline activities, and requesting support when necessary (NIMH, 2023).

Cognitive Behavioral Therapy (CBT): An effective method for tackling social media addiction is cognitive behavioral therapy (CBT). This treatment method has shown notable advantages for adolescents dealing with excessive use of social media. CBT assists individuals in recognizing and modifying unhealthy thought processes and behaviors linked to their online activities. By promoting more flexible thinking, CBT helps teenagers identify the triggers for their social media usage and cultivate healthier coping methods. By engaging in this process, they can develop the ability to control their impulses and make more deliberate decisions about their online interactions, thereby lessening the adverse effects of social media on their lives.

Mindfulness and Self-Regulation: Alongside CBT, methods like mindfulness training and self-regulation strategies have also been effective in addressing social media addiction. Mindfulness techniques promote greater awareness of one's thoughts, emotions, and actions in the current moment. This increased awareness can assist teenagers in identifying when they are participating in compulsive social media usage and enable them to stop and consider their decisions. Strategies for self-regulation, such as establishing clear boundaries on social media usage and assigning specific "offline" periods, help adolescents cultivate a balanced interaction with technology. Collectively, these methods enable adolescents to manage their social media usage and enhance their overall health.

References

1. American Psychological Association. (2024). Teens are spending nearly 5 hours daily on social media. Here are the mental health outcomes. https://www.apa.org/monitor/2024/04/teen-social-use-mental-health
2. National Institute of Mental Health. (2023). Mental illness. https://www.nimh.nih.gov/health/statistics/mental-illness
3. John A Naslund et al. (2020). Social Media and Mental Health: Benefits, Risks, and Opportunities for Research and Practice. J Technol Behav Sci.; 5(3):245–257. doi: 10.1007/s41347-020-00134-x
1.

XVI
Coping With Stress and Depression

"Mental pain is less dramatic than physical pain, but it is more common and also more hard to bear. The frequent attempt to conceal mental pain increases the burden: it is easier to say "My tooth is aching" than to say 'My heart is broken.'"

— C.S. Lewis

The influence of stress on the onset and progress of depression can be viewed as the outcome of various overlapping factors, such as the ongoing impact of environmental stressors and the enduring consequences of stressful childhood experiences, both of which can lead to sustained hyperactivity of the hypothalamic-pituitary-adrenal axis. Stress is the body's reaction to physical or emotional pressures. Emotional strain can contribute to the onset of depression or serve as one of its symptoms. A stressful circumstance may evoke feelings of depression, and such feelings can hinder the ability to cope with stress. Experiencing the loss of a family member, going through a divorce, and relocating are significant life events that can lead to stress. Certain studies associate an overactive stress response and elevated cortisol levels in the body with depression and various health issues, such as heart disease. When the brain perceives danger, the body releases increased levels of stress hormones like cortisol to assist in combating or fleeing from the threat. This is effective in situations of real danger, but it may not always be advantageous in your everyday life.

The World Health Organization (WHO) reports that nearly 280 million individuals suffer from depression worldwide. Depression is described as "a serious mood disorder that leads to symptoms influencing how you feel, think, and manage everyday tasks, like sleeping, eating, or working." People might identify it through ongoing sadness and disinterest in activities they once liked. Although depression manifests in various ways, here are two of the most prevalent depressive disorders linked to chronic stress. At present, the WHO forecasts that by 2030, depression will become the foremost cause of disease burden globally. Depression can affect anyone regardless of age, gender, race or ethnicity, income, culture, or education. Research suggests that genetic, biological, environmental, and psychological factors play a role in the disorder.

The Stress-Depression Connection

Stress is like carrying a heavy backpack; at first, we don't notice its burden and keep pushing forward. But, over time, as more items are added to the bag – such as responsibilities and worries – the load becomes heavier and increasingly difficult to manage. Stress and depression are linked, and stressful life events can trigger depressive episodes. Stress can lead to depression through several factors, including inflammation, neurotransmitter changes, and altered brain activity. "We think that the causal relationship between stress and depression is what's called 'bidirectional," Prescott says. "One can cause the other, and the other can cause the first, and both can make each other worse."

"Depression disrupts your life, so you often are more isolated," Prescott says. "Sometimes you shrink your interpersonal network and stop doing a lot of activities, like work or school or things that you enjoy. We know that kind of isolation makes your perceived stress level go up, so we know that depression can cause stress." "A severe stress, like a divorce or a huge financial change, is a major stressor, and it sends the psyche sort of out of equilibrium. If you keep raising levels of stress, something's going to happen, and often it is depression," Landau says.

How Stress Can Lead to Depression

- **Stressful Experiences:** Chronic stress and stressful childhood experiences can cause long-term changes in the brain.
- **Inflammation:** Stress can cause inflammation in the brain and body, which can contribute to depression.
- **Neurotransmitter Changes:** Stress can cause changes in the levels of neurotransmitters like serotonin, dopamine, and norepinephrine.
- **Brain Activity Changes:** Stress can cause changes in the activity of the amygdala and hippocampus, which can contribute to depression.

The consequences of chronic or prolonged stress can be damaging by themselves, yet they can also lead to depression, a mood disorder that induces feelings of sadness and a lack of interest in activities you typically find enjoyable. Depression may impact your eating habits, your sleeping patterns, and your capacity to focus. Persistent stress can slowly deteriorate an individual's outlook, leading to heightened negativity and resentment. These impacts may subsequently create an opportunity for depression to develop. Moreover, people with existing mental health conditions are at a greater risk of experiencing increased stress than those who do not have such issues. Research has indicated a strong connection between stress and depression. This chain reaction is, luckily, reversible with appropriate treatment and attention.

Managing Stress: Stress is a common and normal occurrence – it's something we all go through occasionally. In moderation, a little stress can boost our motivation and help us accomplish tasks. Nonetheless, when stress becomes overwhelming or persists for an extended period, it can influence our daily routines and even impact our physical and mental well-being. Completely removing stress is just not a feasible option. New problems and challenges will continually arise in everyday life. Nonetheless, opting to handle these stresses more positively can significantly lessen the effects they may have on an individual's physical and mental well-being. Furthermore, this action contributes to lowering the chances of experiencing depression.

Physical health

- *Sleep*: Get enough sleep, ideally 7–9 hours per night. Try to go to bed and wake up at the same time each day.
- *Exercise*: Move more, even a little bit at a time.
- *Eat Well*: Eat a balanced diet with fruits, vegetables, lean protein, whole grains, and healthy fats.
- *Limit Unhealthy Substances*: Avoid smoking, vaping, and excessive alcohol and caffeine.

Mental health

- *Practice Self-Care*: Do things that are meaningful to you, like meditation or relaxation.
- *Be Kind to Yourself*: Don't think hurtful things about yourself.
- *Identify Negative Thoughts*: Challenge unhelpful thoughts and try to see problems differently.
- *Build Emotional Strength*: Stay connected with friends and family, and have a positive outlook

Recognizing when stress becomes an issue is the initial step in identifying its impact on your life and exploring proactive approaches for managing it. In doing this, you can act before it results in issues for mental and physical well-being. Mindfulness as a method for managing stress is an easy technique that can be done anywhere, at any moment. Studies have indicated that mindfulness meditation may help alleviate the impacts of stress-related issues, including anxiety, insomnia, lack of focus, and low spirits. Engage with others. Take some time with a friend or relative who will hear you out. It serves as a natural method to soothe you and reduce your stress. When you interact with others face-to-face, your body produces a hormone that halts your fight-or-flight reaction.

Treating Depression

Without properly managing daily stress, depression can easily slip in and take root. When depression is not tended to, the effects can deepen and lead to additional mental health issues. Most distressingly, the risk of suicide increases with the worsening of symptoms as well as deeper levels of sorrow. Seeking treatment is a crucial step in preventing chronic stress from developing into depression and saving lives. Fortunately, depression can be treated, and programs are available to build a happy and fulfilled life again. The most common form of treatment for depression, whether stress-induced or otherwise, is psychotherapy. During this form of treatment, people are encouraged to change their perspectives of different situations.

Psychotherapy: Psychotherapy is a general term for treating depression by talking about your condition and related issues with a mental health professional. There are several different types of psychological treatments including:

- Cognitive Behaviour Therapy (CBT)
- Interpersonal Therapy (IPT)
- Behaviour Therapy

- Mindfulness-Based Cognitive Therapy (MBCT).

CBT is among the most frequently utilized psychological treatments. It assists individuals with depression in tracking and altering negative thought patterns while enhancing their coping abilities, making them more prepared to handle life's pressures and challenges.

Medication

- **Ketamine:** An anesthetic drug that can help with treatment-resistant depression.
- **Brain Stimulation Therapy**: Electroconvulsive therapy (ECT), transcranial magnetic stimulation (TMS), and vagus nerve stimulation (VNS) are all types of brain stimulation therapy that can help treat depression.
- **Selective serotonin reuptake inhibitors (SSRIs):** Physicians typically begin treatment by recommending an SSRI. These medications are regarded as safer and typically result in fewer annoying side effects compared to other categories of antidepressants. SSRIs consist of citalopram (Celexa), escitalopram (Lexapro), fluoxetine (Prozac), paroxetine (Paxil, Pexeva), sertraline (Zoloft), and vilazodone (Viibryd).
- **Serotonin-norepinephrine reuptake inhibitors (SNRIs):** Examples of SNRIs include duloxetine (Cymbalta), venlafaxine (Effexor XR), desvenlafaxine (Pristiq, Khedezla) and levomilnacipran (Fetzima).
- **Atypical Antidepressants:** These drugs do not align clearly with any of the other categories of antidepressants. Included are bupropion (Wellbutrin XL, Wellbutrin SR, Aplenzin, Forfivo XL), mirtazapine (Remeron), nefazodone, trazodone, and vortioxetine (Trintellix).
- **Tricyclic Antidepressants**: These medications — including imipramine (Tofranil), nortriptyline (Pamelor), amitriptyline,

doxepin, trimipramine (Surmontil), desipramine (Norpramin), and protriptyline (Vivactil) — can be highly effective, but often lead to more severe side effects compared to newer antidepressants. Tricyclics typically aren't recommended unless you've first used an SSRI without seeing any improvement.

- **Monoamine oxidase inhibitors (MAOIs):** MAOIs — like tranylcypromine (Parnate), phenelzine (Nardil), and isocarboxazid (Marplan) — may be recommended, usually when other medications are ineffective, due to their potential for serious side effects. Taking MAOIs necessitates a rigid diet due to perilous (or potentially fatal) interactions with certain foods — like specific cheeses, pickles, and wines — as well as some medicines and herbal supplements. Selegiline (Emsam), a more recent MAOI that adheres to the skin as a patch, might result in fewer side effects compared to other MAOIs. These drugs cannot be used alongside SSRIs.

- **Other medications.** Additional medications might be included with an antidepressant to boost its effects. Your physician might suggest using two antidepressants together or incorporating other medications like mood stabilizers or antipsychotics. Short-term use of anti-anxiety and stimulant medications may also be incorporated.

Although psychological and medical care can aid in recovery, there are numerous other methods individuals can use to improve themselves and maintain well-being. When experiencing depression, you might find that activities you used to love no longer to bring you joy. You might believe you won't like something, yet when you try it, you find you enjoy it even more than anticipated. Depression can interfere with sleep routines. Restoring a regular sleep pattern is crucial for a complete recovery. It is typical for individuals with depression to feel anxious or have negative thoughts. This influences your capacity to concentrate on recovery and renders you more susceptible to negative feelings. Note down your concerns. Examine every worry and consider the realism of your negative beliefs. Investigate different ideas and interpretations. Evaluate if it was successful in addressing the issue.

ॐ

References

1. Hyman S.E. (2007). How mice cope with stressful social situations. Cell;131(2): 232–234. doi: 10.1016/j.cell.2007.10.008.
2. Yannick Griep et al. (2023). Feeling stressed and depressed? A three-wave follow-up study of the beneficial effects of voluntary work; 23(3): 100363. https://doi.org/10.1016/j.ijchp.2022.100363
3. LeMoult, J. (2020). From Stress to Depression: Bringing Together Cognitive and Biological Science. Current Directions in Psychological Science, 29(6), 592-598. https://doi.org/10.1177/0963721420964039

XVII

A Guide to Motivation

"It always seems impossible until it's done." — Nelson Mandela
"Success is not final; failure is not fatal: It is the courage to continue that counts." —Winston Churchill

Motivation is described as the process that starts, directs, and sustains goal-directed behaviors. Motivation drives us to act, whether that's grabbing a glass of water to quench our thirst or reading a book to acquire knowledge. It encompasses the biological, emotional, social, and cognitive influences that drive behavior. In common language, the word motivation is often employed to explain why someone engages in an activity. Motivation is a key aspect of human behavior that drives individuals to undertake the actions required to reach their personal and career objectives. It can assist you in seeking valuable chances that could promote your career growth and foster significant skills. Grasping how to foster motivation can equip you with the encouragement needed to complete tasks and establish goals for yourself.

How Does Motivation Work?

Motivation refers to the drive to act toward achieving a goal. Therefore, it is crucial to establish and accomplish our objectives. It's an essential human requirement that aids our survival and engagement with the world.

- **Brain chemistry:** The brain releases neurotransmitters such as dopamine when you undergo a pleasurable or rewarding experience. This enhances your drive to keep seeking comparable results.
- **Neural pathways:** Repeated behaviors create more efficient neural pathways in the brain.
- **Reward circuitry:** The brain's reward circuitry, which includes the prefrontal cortex and nucleus accumbens, helps you set goals, plan actions, and evaluate rewards.
- **Motivation types:** There are two main types of motivation: intrinsic and extrinsic. Intrinsic motivation comes from within you, while extrinsic motivation comes from outside you.
- **Reinforcement theory:** This theory states that behaviors that are followed by positive outcomes are more likely to be repeated.

Motivation relies on recognizing the individual and knowing what is important to them. The reality is that every form of motivation originates from within oneself. When people inspire us, they are simply helping us tap into what is significant to us and the necessity of acting. The fundamental question frequently found at the core of motivation is the question of WHY. You inquire about 'why' to help the individual connect with their fundamental values and motivations for acting. However, that isn't sufficient. Motivation isn't just about choosing to complete a task. It involves choosing to prioritize one task over others. It suggests that we give preference to one thing over another. That frequently obstructs most motivation efforts. You must grasp what the different key tasks are that must be completed and when they should be accomplished.

A Guide to Motivation: A guide to motivation can include tips for setting goals, understanding motivation theories, and identifying what drives a person.

Setting goals

- **Set clear goals:** Set goals that are specific and measurable so you can track your progress.
- **Break goals into smaller steps:** Set mini goals to build momentum and make it easier to achieve your larger goals.
- **Reward yourself:** Reward yourself for both small and big wins

Understanding motivation theories

- **Maslow's Hierarchy of Needs:** This theory suggests that people have five layers of needs, and they must satisfy the lower needs before they can address the higher needs.
- **McClelland's Theory of Needs:** This theory suggests that people are motivated by one of three needs: achievement, affiliation, or power.
- **Herzberg's Two-Factor Theory:** This theory suggests that people are motivated by things that make them happy at work, like recognition and achievements, and things that keep them from being unhappy, like a good work environment and fair pay.
- **Expectancy Theory:** This theory suggests that people are more likely to perform certain behaviors if they believe those actions will lead to desirable outcomes.

Identifying What Drives a Person: To determine what motivates an individual, you may reflect on their values, passions, abilities, and experiences. You can also examine the activities they like and the goals they wish to reach. Motivation can be felt as coming from within. Biological factors arise from an individual's brain and nervous system, while psychological factors reflect aspects of a person's mind, including their psychological needs.

External motivational sources are frequently perceived through environmental factors, such as incentives or objectives. Our internal motivational sources combine with external influences to guide behavior (Deckers, 2014). Physiological needs—such as hunger, thirst, and sex—are the biological foundations that ultimately express themselves as psychological motivations. These biological occurrences turn into psychological drives. It is vital to differentiate the physiological necessity from the psychological urge it generates, as only the latter possess motivational characteristics.

Drive Motivation: When the sympathetic nervous system generates epinephrine and norepinephrine, it creates power for activity. This could explain why motivation is frequently understood about drives. Our bodies seek to achieve balance and work towards a preferred outcome, minimizing or removing the motivation (Reeve, 2018). Needs are intrinsic drives that motivate, guide, and maintain actions. They produce efforts essential for sustaining life, development, and health.

"A hungry stomach will not allow its owner to forget it, whatever his cares and sorrows."

-Homer, 800 B.C.

- **Goal Motivation:** When discussing motivation, goals inevitably arise. A goal, as a cognitive mental occurrence, acts as a "spring to action" that drives us, energizing and guiding our behavior in intentional ways, and encouraging individuals to act differently (Ames & Ames, 1984). Goals, like mindset, beliefs, expectations, and self-concept, are sources of internal motives. These cognitive sources of motivation unite and spring us into action.
- Goals are generated by what is NOT, or in other words, a discrepancy between where we are and where we want to be. The saying "If you don't know where you're going, any road will get you there" describes the difference in motivated behavior between those who have goals and those who do not (Locke, 1996; Locke & Latham, 1990, 2002).

Motivation and Emotion: The concept of motivation is closely related to emotion. Both words are derived from the same underlying Latin root move which means "to move."

- Emotions are considered motivational states because they generate bursts of energy that get our attention and cause our reactions to significant events in our lives (Izard, 1993).

- Emotions generate an impulse to cope with the circumstances at hand (Keltner & Gross, 1999).

Along with emotion, motivation constitutes a fundamental psychological phenomenon known as affect. We experience these events, both physically and emotionally, which in turn inspire and direct our actions and choices. Above all, they greatly influence our mental and physical well-being.

Motivation and Personality: Personality theories and studies indicate that our motivations vary according to our personality traits. A strong presence of a specific trait frequently influences our behavior per that trait: We tend to be more open to experiences, responsible, sociable, friendly, and anxious. We will be driven by various incentives, objectives, and pursuits, yet we will also opt to be in distinct circumstances.

- The cybernetic big five theory links personality traits with the type of goals we choose and shows that specific goals would motivate appropriate personality state behaviors that are effective for achieving that goal (Deckers, 2014).
- Personality traits of conscientiousness, openness, and extraversion have been positively associated with intrinsic motivation. Conscientiousness, extraversion, and neuroticism on the other hand have been positively related to extrinsic achievement motivation (Deckers, 2014).

Motivation for Change: A few of us enroll in a gym or a training course; others seek therapy or coaching because we wish for transformation. However, transformation is seldom an uncomplicated or straightforward process. One reason relates to the challenge of discovering the drive to participate in tasks that lack inherent motivation. In this context, motivation rises alongside the readiness for change, which is influenced by our: Willingness to change, Confidence in achieving the desired change, and the Actions we take to implement the change.

- Deci and Ryan (1995), who studied autonomous self-regulation, suggested that we need to move away from extrinsically motivated action, (e.g., when we must do something because we fear consequences), and toward introjected and even fully self-determined regulation, where we value the new behavior and align it with other aspects of our life.
- "Stage-based" approaches to behavioral changes have proven to be particularly effective in increasing motivation toward the pursuit of difficult and non-intrinsically motivating goals as they allow for realistic expectations of progress (Zimmerman, Olsen, & Bosworth, 2000).
- The Stages of Change model of Prochaska, et al. (DiClemente, & Prochaska, 1998), also known as the Trans-theoretical Model of Change (TMC), is a prevalent method utilized in clinical environments. In this model, change is seen as slow, step-by-step, and manageable. Its practical uses are evident in motivational interviewing techniques, a client-focused approach to encouraging change.

Grasping the concepts of motivation empowers us to discover effective solutions for actual motivational issues. What could be more crucial than enabling those around us to take more deliberate actions, achieve their goals, enjoy optimal experiences, function fully, develop healthily, and cultivate a resilient self-identity? Examining and utilizing motivational science can assist us in overcoming or managing impulsive desires, routine behaviors, goal setbacks, ineffective functioning, negative feelings, ennui, harmful or dysfunctional growth, and a vulnerable self-concept. If the greatest victory is over self, should we not aspire to rise above our limitations?

References

- Deckers, L. (2014). Motivation: Biological, psychological, and environmental (4th ed.). Boston, MA: Allyn & Bacon.
- Graef, R., Csikszentmihalyi, M., & Gianinno, S. M. (1983). Measuring intrinsic motivation in everyday life. Leisure Studies, 2, 155–168. https://doi.org/10.1080/02614368300390121
- Lawrence, P. R., & Nohria, N. (2002). Driven: How human nature shapes our choices. John Wiley & Sons.
- Locke, E. A. (1996). Motivation through conscious goal setting. Applied & Preventive Psychology, 5, 117-124. https://doi.org/10.1016/S0962-1849(96)80005-9

XVIII

The Unconscious Mind

The unconscious mind is frequently regarded by numerous psychological researchers as merely a shadow of a "real" conscious mind; however, there is now considerable evidence suggesting that the unconscious is not less flexible, complex, controlling, deliberative, or action-oriented than its counterpart. The 'Unconscious Mind' pertains to the aspect of our mental processes that function without our conscious recognition. It is thought to contribute to problem-solving and creative thought, persisting on a task even when our conscious mind cannot identify a solution. Nonetheless, contemporary cognitive science recognizes that all cognitive functions operate unconsciously, and the notion of the 'unconscious mind' does not adequately clarify these processes. The unconscious mind may encompass suppressed emotions, concealed memories, routines, thoughts, wishes, and responses. Memories and feelings that are excessively painful, embarrassing, shameful, or distressing to confront consciously are held in the vast reservoir comprised of the unconscious mind.

- The unconscious mind is the repository of forgotten memories.

- It's the source of automatic thoughts that appear without any apparent cause.
- It's the locus of implicit knowledge, which is things that we have learned so well that we do them without thinking.
- The unconscious mind is often viewed as the shadow of the conscious mind.
- The unconscious mind is not less complex than the conscious mind, and it can be controlling, deliberative, and action-oriented.

According to Freud (1915), The subconscious mind is the main origin of human actions. Like an iceberg, the crucial section of the mind is the segment that remains invisible. In psychoanalysis, the unconscious mind denotes the segment of the psyche that holds suppressed thoughts and images, along with basic desires and impulses that have always been kept from entering the conscious mind. Freud's theory of personality in psychoanalysis describes the unconscious mind as a storehouse for thoughts, emotions, desires, and memories.

- **Thoughts:** Unconscious thoughts include feelings, urges, and memories.
- **Beliefs:** The unconscious mind stores beliefs and values.
- **Memories:** The unconscious mind determines memories.
- **Defense Mechanisms:** The unconscious mind uses defense mechanisms to reduce internal stress.

The unconscious holds various important and troubling content that we must keep from our awareness because they are too dangerous to recognize completely. Freud also thought that all our fundamental instincts and impulses were held within the unconscious mind. The instincts of life and death, for instance, were discovered within the unconscious. The life instincts, often referred to as the sexual instincts, are those connected to survival. The instincts of death encompass thoughts related to aggression, trauma, and threats.

Are Freud and Psychoanalysis Still Relevant?

Modern psychologists hold diverse opinions on Freud's concept of the unconscious mind; some acknowledge its existence, while others dispute it. Setting aside the issue of the repression of distressing content in the unconscious, a significant portion of contemporary cognitive psychology and neuroscience aligns with the Freudian perspective that behavior can become automatic through repeated practice and that the regulation of such behavior is transferred to independent or partially independent unconscious systems. Contemporary theories regarding facial expressiveness, for instance, clearly acknowledge the influence of both conscious and unconscious behavior regulation (Ekman, 1986).

It's crucial to keep in mind that psychoanalysis aims to uncover deeper understandings of an individual's mind, which contrasts significantly with our current perspective on the practice and application of psychoanalysis and psychotherapy. Particularly for professionals in the field who are involved in the actual process, the concepts of id, ego, and superego breakdown along with dream analysis represent overly simplistic methods and notions that are unlikely to effectively tackle the challenges modern mental health care aims to resolve. Numerous methods, techniques, and conclusions of Freud have been challenged to the extent that some of his theories are regarded as harmful—and potentially perilous—to specific groups, including his perspectives on women and homosexuality.

While Freud (1915) saw the unconscious as one unified entity, psychology today recognizes the mind as a set of modules that have developed over time and function beyond conscious awareness. Freud thought that primitive impulses stayed unconscious to shield people from anxiety, whereas contemporary views of the adaptive unconscious suggest that most information processing occurs outside awareness for efficiency instead of repression (Wilson,

2004).

Finally, Freud's contemporary insights relate more to perspectives rather than specific therapeutic techniques, though this is not negative. He set up the foundations upon which contemporary mental health care is based, and the current mindset of those involved in the mental health care process appears to originate from his central thesis regarding what patients ought to gain from therapy, which can be summed up as, "Know thyself."

For more information Read

1. Mardoche Sidor, (2024). The Impact of Unconscious Motives on Human Behavior: A Deep Dive into Freudian Theory. https://sweetinstitute.com/the-impact-of-unconscious-motives-on-human-behavior-a-deep-dive-into-freudian-theory/
2. John A Bargh (2019). The modern unconscious. World Psychiatry; 18(2):225–226. doi: https://doi.org/10.1002/wps.20625
3. Ellenberger, H. F. (1970). The discovery of the unconscious: The history and evolution of dynamic psychiatry. New York: Basic Books.
4. Gay, P. (1988). Freud: A life for our time. London: Dent.
5. Weiskrantz, L. (1997). Consciousness lost and found: A neuropsychological exploration. Oxford: Oxford University Press.

XIX

Understanding Tribal Psychology

Just as a picture is separated into figure and ground, we also classify the social world into us and them. What is the cause of that? The tribal mindset seen in individuals is an important trait for evolution, but the growing tribal divisions seriously threaten our individualistic society. What is the origin of this tribal psychology? Were there challenges that could have been addressed, at least to some extent, by employing tribal psychology? There are three main categories for evolutionary explanations. Psychologists Lilliana Mason and Dan Kahan credit Tribal Psychology and the amplifying influence of social media for the increase in political polarization. Recognizing individuals from different tribes had advantages for safety in terms of evolution. Small, illogical discrepancies can easily deceive our minds into incorporating or disregarding something. The brain is crucial in molding cognitive, emotional, and social abilities. One of the brain's fascinating characteristics is its natural inclination towards social connections. Human beings naturally flourish in social environments and actively pursue relationships with one another. Neuroscientists have thoroughly researched this phenomenon and pinpointed different neural mechanisms that are the basis of our social behavior. The brain's tribal instincts are a result of the crucial role social behavior plays in human survival and evolution. Our predecessors resided in tiny clusters, requiring collaboration, structure, and the cultivation of social abilities like communication, empathy, and cooperation, all of which offered a competitive edge in terms of natural selection.

Tribal Psychology

The tribe exists within our consciousness. It is the inner psychological representation of the plural pronoun "us". It is always defined as its opposite, "them". The tribe is an artificial creation of society. Creating the tribe collectively helps form and structure our perspective on the world. Tribal psychology involves humans' inclination to create social groups and connect with them, rooted in common values, objectives, and sense of self. The natural inclination of the human brain to form social connections is a crucial evolutionary trait. Certain aspects of tribal psychology involve recognizing the difference between those within the group and those outside of it, showing strong fondness for members of the group, and feeling hostility towards disloyal group members. Tribalism can be beneficial by fostering group commitment among individuals. Nevertheless, tribalism can result in bullying and is considered a threat to individualistic societies. Research in social psychology shows that humans have a strong tribal psychology, which includes behaviors such as favoring ingroup members, developing strong bonds with ingroups, disliking disloyal ingroup members, and engaging in discrimination.

Tribal identity imbues individuals with a positive self-perception. This is crucial for the mental well-being of the tribe. Every tribe depicts itself using the most elevated language. The tribe instructs its members that their people are the most intelligent, powerful, truthful, and attractive individuals, shaping both the tribe's identity and that of its members with these positive images of the group. Carl Jung refers to this embellished, magnified, inflated self-image as the "exalted self". We shall name it the Majestic Clannish Self. This is the tribal equivalent of the Jungian concept of the Persona, where individuals present only their most positive traits to the world.

Tribes place a high importance on unity, consensus, and togetherness above all else. This is instilled and nurtured in the minds of every tribal member starting at a young age. The tribe suppresses disagreement, especially concerning other tribes, but dissent and innovation are heavily restricted in tribal communities. No other social system is as traditional as a tribal community. The tribe's lasting existence and its outdated values are due to the stifling of opposing viewpoints. Watching this phenomenon unfold is truly remarkable. Members of the tribe reach an agreement on national matters so quickly that one might question if the tribal shared consciousness goes beyond time and distance. This is how groupthink is manifested in the workplace. Tribal members do not need discussion papers or consensus-building conferences to agree on their opinions. They share a common belief that allows them to easily and instinctively develop a similar viewpoint.

The Characteristics of Tribal Psychology

As creatures who thrive in groups, we have an innate "desire for connection." Even if we are unaware of it, we may still possess this need, which is nestled deep within us. The significance of addressing our need for belonging to a group is that it has practical implications for our emotional well-being, not just a theoretical concept. The renowned Swiss psychologist Carl Gustav Jung might have been unaware of Somali tribes. Out of all the psychological theories, his constructs most accurately portray tribal psychology, including the collective unconscious, archetypes, persona, and shadow. The community resides within the shared subconscious of its members. A sense of tribal identity boosts members' self-esteem. This is crucial for the mental well-being of the tribe. Some psychological benefits of belonging to a Tribal Community are listed below:

- Belonging to a tribal identity helps members develop a positive self-image. Being part of a group and feeling connected to fellow group members is crucial for our sense of identity and self-esteem.
- Group identity often leads to a shared sense of purpose when working towards collective objectives.
- Not only are they willing to accept help from community members, but they also consider it more valuable and meaningful. This happens when we believe that people within our group are better at comprehending our feelings, making their encouragement and approval more effective than that of outsiders.
- Becoming part of a community with individuals who have similar interests or goals can help boost our social interactions. We tend to feel a stronger bond with individuals who have the same purpose or passion as us, and as a result, they are more likely to embrace and include us due to this shared bond.

The tribal instincts hypothesis has many predictions about the evolved psychological mechanisms behind intergroup behavior in humans. Tribes have similar thoughts. Tribes have similar political viewpoints. There is no principle on which the political support of a tribe is grounded. It is transient and changing like the sand in the desert. Tribal Selective Information Filter is possibly the most widespread and harmful feature of tribal psychopathology. The mental mechanism known as the Selective Information Filter is deeply rooted in the minds of tribe members. The tribe views information about the world based on their self-interest, caring about how it affects them rather than others. Members actively choose to sieve through information about different tribal groups. People in the tribal group are unaware of the successes and failures of others, experiencing a significant lack of knowledge. Studies in anthropology show that revenge is the primary reason behind tribal conflicts. Tribes do not engage in conflict based on principles. They struggle to seek revenge. A tribal group is committed to protecting the dignity and sacredness of their own lives and to attacking their enemies. Tribal conflict is intimate. It is instantaneous. It evokes emotions. And it is unattractive. Seeking vengeance is a difficult motive that is fueled by emotions. It retains memories over a long period. Furthermore, revenge requires more than just fairness, more than just retribution. The victim of the vengeance must be shown a lesson. He needs to understand unequivocally how incorrect he was to challenge this tribe.

Globally, mental disorders are rising with increasing urbanization. India has the world's second-largest tribal population, and it is critical to appreciate the mental health problems in this population. However, the extent of mental health issues among tribal populations is unknown. Social determinants are key risk factors associated with mental disorders, more particularly among disadvantaged tribal populations. Knowledge about mental health in the community, stigma, effective strategies to specifically approach and interact with this population in providing mental health care, and the acceptability and feasibility of different mental health service delivery modalities in these communities need to be well-researched and understood, before scaling up services.

References and For Further Reading

1. Cory J. Clark et al. (2019). Tribalism Is Human Nature. https://cpb-us-e2.wpmucdn.com/sites.uci.edu/dist/1/863/files/2019/10/Clark-et-al-2019.pdf
2. Van Vugt, M. & H. Park, Justin. The Tribal Instinct Hypothesis: Evolution and the Social Psychology of Intergroup Relations. https://www.researchgate.net/publication/329183431

3. M. Schaller, J. A. Simpson, & D. T. Kenrick (2010), Evolution and social psychology. New York: Psychology Press.

4. Rao Palkansh., Kalpana Jain., Anita Manglani (2022). A Comparative Analysis of Mindset and Psychological Capital for Tribal and Non-Tribal Adolescents. Bulletin of the American Schools of Oriental Research XCI-XLIX(1):42-55.

XX

The Psychology of Forgiveness

"Forgiveness may be the best hope for our rage-filled world. In a lively style, Kenneth Briggs deftly explores the tough questions and illuminates the transforming power of forgiveness."

-Donald B. Kraybill

Forgiveness holds various meanings for various individuals. However, it typically requires a conscious choice to release feelings of resentment and anger. Forgiveness can be seen as substituting negative feelings towards an offender with positive ones. Pardoning someone who has harmed you is always challenging, but continuously ruminating on those incidents and experiencing them repeatedly can saturate your mind with harmful thoughts and bottled-up resentment. However, once you master the art of forgiveness, you will not be constrained by the previous deeds of others and will truly experience freedom. Engaging in forgiveness can offer significant health advantages. Observational studies, along with certain randomized trials, indicate that forgiveness correlates with decreased levels of depression, anxiety, and hostility; less substance abuse; improved self-esteem; and increased life satisfaction. It is only by forgiving that we can attain genuine freedom and happiness in life.

Forgiveness does not imply forgetting or justifying the injury caused to you. It also doesn't automatically imply reconciling with the individual who inflicted the damage. Forgiveness offers a sense of tranquility that enables you to concentrate on yourself and assists you in moving forward with life. Forgiving someone means letting go of negative feelings tied to a past action, but it doesn't imply that you fully forget the memory of that event; you can forgive someone without erasing what they did. Forgiveness is an undertaking that demands time and perseverance. Forgiveness does not imply that you wipe away the past or overlook what occurred. It doesn't necessarily mean that the other individual will alter their behavior -- you are unable to influence that. It simply signifies that you are releasing the anger and hurt and progressing toward a more positive situation.

- **Forgiveness Is Emotional Release:** When you forgive someone, you choose to let go of anger, resentment, and the desire for revenge, allowing you to move forward emotionally.
- **Forgetting Is Memory Erasure:** Forgetting means the memory of an event is completely gone from your mind.
- **You Can Forgive Without Forgetting:** It's possible to forgive someone for their actions while still remembering what happened.

If you're struggling to start the process, recognize and express the aspects you wish to forgive. Frequently, pain and grievances become tangled and mixed. They might not even originate from the same source. Begin the process by clearly identifying what you wish to forgive. Pardoning is a journey. Letting go of anger and resentment can truly be an expression of self-kindness.... Anticipating [forgiveness] as a one-time event—driven solely by the need to move forward and forget—can be more harmful than the initial feelings of anger. The next level of forgiveness is outward: centering on our sense of thankfulness for the insights we gain throughout our journey.... [Forgiveness] involves recognizing the grievance alongside the emotions it generates, understanding that individuals are hurt, imperfect, and chaotic including myself, establishing suitable boundaries, releasing attachments, and progressing forward.

REACH Method

A highly effective approach to practicing forgiveness is through the REACH method. REACH is an acronym for Recall, Emphasize, Altruistic Gift, Commit, and Hold. Here is an overview of every stage.

- **Recall:** The initial step is to remember the misdeed impartially. The aim is not to view the person negatively or indulge in self-pity, but to achieve a clear grasp of the wrongdoing that occurred. Envision the individual and the circumstances along with all the emotions that accompany them. Don't ignore anything, particularly if it triggers feelings of anger or sadness.
- **Empathize:** Next, attempt to comprehend the other individual's perspective on why they caused you pain while avoiding belittling or diminishing the wrongdoing that occurred. Occasionally, the misbehavior wasn't directed at anyone but stemmed from issues the other individual was facing. "Individuals who aggress against others are occasionally experiencing their feelings of fear, concern, and pain." "They frequently fail to consider their actions when causing pain to others, and instead, they react impulsively."
- **Altruistic Gift:** This phase involves confronting your deficiencies. Remember an occasion when you were unkind to someone, and they forgave you. What emotions did it evoke in you? Understanding this allows you to see that forgiveness is a selfless present you can offer to others.
- **Commit:** Devote yourself to forgiving. For example, document your forgiveness in a journal, compose an unsent letter, or share

it with a friend. "This aids in the decision-making aspect of forgiveness."

- **Hold:** Ultimately, cling to your forgiveness. This stage is challenging as recollections of the event frequently resurface. "Forgiveness does not mean forgetting." "Instead, it's about altering how you respond to those memories."

When negative emotions come up, remind yourself that you have granted forgiveness and ultimately wish well for the person who wronged you. If necessary, review your dedication by looking back at your journal entries or letters, or by remembering the discussion you had with a friend.

Personality and Forgiveness

Individuals who are forgiving vary from those who are less forgiving across numerous personality traits. For instance, those who forgive others experience reduced negative impacts like anxiety, depression, and anger. People who are forgiving tend to be less prone to rumination, less focused on themselves, less exploitative and exhibit greater empathy than those who are not as forgiving. Those who forgive often support attitudes and behaviors that are viewed positively in society. In the Big Five personality framework (e.g., John & Srivastava, 1999), the tendency to forgive seems to be most closely associated with agreeableness and neuroticism (McCullough & Hoyt, 1999). Consequently, the forgiving individual seems to be a person who is quite high in agreeableness and somewhat low in neuroticism/negative emotionality.

- Mahatma Gandhi - "The weak can never forgive; forgiveness is an attribute of the strong"
- Worthington and Scherer (2004) inability to forgive in our daily life is the main root of psychological suffering.

It is viewed as a crucial element for maintaining smooth and healthy relationships with others, as it greatly impacts individuals' physical and mental well-being. Individuals who hold onto grudges create many challenges for themselves and others, making it hard for them to sustain their relationships. Thus, it is essential to investigate which personality traits are more inclined to forgive.

Social Factors Influencing Forgiveness

Forgiveness is also affected by the nature of wrongdoings and the situations in which they take place. Typically, individuals find it harder to pardon wrongdoings that appear more deliberate, and serious, and result in greater negative outcomes. Cultural, age-related, racial, gender-based, and individualism-collectivism social factors affect forgiveness.

- **Individualism-collectivism:** How cultures think about individuals versus groups can influence how people think about forgiveness.
- **Openness to new ideas:** How open societies are to new ideas can influence forgiveness.
- **Traditional beliefs and norms:** How traditional societies are in terms of their beliefs and norms can influence forgiveness.

Forgiveness, Health, and Well-Being

Forgiveness involves releasing resentment and animosity. It can enhance your mental and physical wellness, resulting in a deeper feeling of well-being. Forgiveness proved to be a gift as it relieved a person from all our internal struggles. In different circumstances, forgiveness reduces depression, enhances our self-worth, and erases previous hurts (Engel, 2001).

- Forgiveness can reduce stress, anxiety, and depression

- It can promote positive emotions and improve self-esteem
- Forgiveness therapy can help with mental health problems
- Forgiveness can improve heart health, lower blood pressure, and improve cholesterol levels
- It can also reduce pain and the risk of heart attack
- Forgiveness can strengthen the immune system
- People who forgive others report higher levels of happiness and well-being
- Forgiveness can lead to healthier relationships

How to practice forgiveness

Forgiveness involves more than merely uttering the phrase. "It's an intentional action where you consciously choose to release negative emotions regardless of whether the individual merits it or not," Swartz explains. When you let go of anger, resentment, and hostility, you start to experience empathy, compassion, and occasionally even fondness for the person who hurt you. Embracing forgiveness means recognizing your emotions, relinquishing control of the circumstance, and deciding to move on from resentments. It may require time, so it's essential to remain patient and deliberate.

Steps for practicing forgiveness

- **Acknowledge your feelings:** Allow yourself to feel hurt, angry, or betrayed without judgment.
- **Identify what needs healing:** Consider who you want to forgive and what you need to heal.
- **Practice empathy:** Try to understand the other person's perspective and emotions.
- **Communicate your feelings:** If you feel comfortable, talk to the person who hurt you.

- **Choose to forgive:** Decide to let go of the control and power that the situation has had on you.
- **Forgive yourself:** Apply the same practices of forgiveness to yourself.
- **Remember change takes time:** Be patient and intentional.

Forgiveness has the power to enhance relationships, lower stress, and anger, and boost happiness and optimism. The individual striving to forgive gains from the act of forgiveness, which alleviates the emotional distress of bitterness—since it pains to be wronged, and it is even more painful to endure both that pain and the subsequent persistent anger.

References

1. Balancing Negative News Reporting: Promoting the Good. Psychology Today. Human Flourishing Blog. June 2020.
2. VanderWeele, T.J. (2018). Is forgiveness a public health issue? American Journal of Public Health, 108:189-190.
3. The Psychology of Forgiveness. Available from: https://www.researchgate.net/publication/ 264443222_The_psychology_of_forgiveness [accessed Jan 18 2025].

XXI

Why do Good People Suffer?

"We could bear nearly any pain or disappointment if we thought there was a reason behind it, a purpose, to it."
— Rabbi Harold Kushner, When Bad Things Happen to Good People.

The Perception of Good Vs. Bad

"People are complicated, and we are all capable of acting wrongly — occasionally for justifiable reasons. Of course, it's equally true that sometimes we do the right things for the wrong reasons."

Exhibiting actions perceived as unusually "bad" can arise from various factors, such as a deficiency in self-awareness. However, this does not always determine a person's identity. The nature of humanity is characterized by flaws. Each person encounters difficulties, commits errors, exercises poor judgment, or utters something they later wish they hadn't. These moments don't define you as a "bad" person; they just reflect your humanity. Being categorized as "good" or "bad" typically originates from how people perceive your consistent behaviors and personality traits. If you generally behave with kindness, empathy, and impartiality, for instance, you might be seen as "good." Being "good," nonetheless, doesn't imply that a person cannot or will not engage in bad actions. By grasping the reasons why good individuals commit wrongdoing, you're nurturing your qualities of kindness, such as empathy and compassion. Traditional behavioral patterns determine how society views a person as "good" or "bad," yet every individual has the potential for both positive and negative deeds. Empathy, kindness, and compassion are typical characteristics observed in individuals who are categorized as "good." Realizing that decent individuals occasionally commit wrong acts can assist you in enhancing those qualities within yourself.

Why Bad Things Happen to Good People?

We exist in a realm of anguish and distress. Everyone is impacted by the tough truths of existence, and the inquiry "Why do bad things occur to good individuals?" stands as one of the most challenging questions ever. As a species that seeks meaning, we often interpret events based on their significance to us: is it beneficial or detrimental? It is a common human tendency to attribute intentional purpose to situations in a self-referential manner. "Why did this occur?" and "Why am I experiencing this?" are thus typical and frequent inquiries made by numerous individuals when confronted with an unexpected negative event, like being diagnosed with cancer. "What have I done to earn this?" "Did I do anything to bring this about?" Numerous individuals tend to question whether they are facing divine punishment for previous wrongdoings or to reflect on whether there exists a secret design or greater purpose behind their hardships, potentially a lesson meant to be learned through their pain. Negative events can occur to decent individuals for numerous reasons, such as the influence of authority figures, the compulsion to fit in, and the inclination to justify poor conduct.

We have the option to act wickedly since free will has been granted to us as a gift. We have the option to drive under the influence and take the lives of innocent pedestrians. Furthermore, we have the option to release harmful substances into the water system, leading to cancer in innocent individuals. We have the option to shoot a gun into the sky without considering where the bullet could fall and whom it might harm or kill. This could clarify numerous global tragedies. A significant amount of suffering can be linked to the harmful or careless actions of other people. Infants may be born with congenital disabilities due to the use of hazardous and radioactive substances in our society. Perhaps those substances and compounds in the environment lead to additional health issues as well.

Theodicy Approach

The theological problem of trying to explain why evil and suffering exist in the world is referred to as theodicy. As hard as it is to acknowledge, we must remember that there are no "good" people, in the absolute sense of the word. All of us are tainted by and infected with sin. As Jesus said, "No one is good—except God alone" (Luke 18:19). All of us feel the effects of sin in one way or another. Another answer is that bad things happen to good people because God allows us to have free will. God in His eternal love has allowed us to do what we want.

The scientific or Non-Theistic Perspective

There is no cosmic purpose or design. Modern science's single most fundamental conclusion is that " the universe has no inherent purpose or design." Yes, as counterintuitive as it is, it is indeed fully plausible that the universe and all the complexity, life, and consciousness contained within it could have emerged and evolved entirely spontaneously and unguided. How precisely this could happen—how such astonishing and 'clever' complexity could have arisen and developed out of fundamental randomness and simplicity (and perhaps ultimately out of nothingness!), is what science is all about.

It's Not Personal

Bad things happen for the same reason anything happens: the same laws of nature that underlie all causes and effects. There is nothing special about the causation of things that we humans judge as "bad." Adopting a secular worldview entails recognizing that meaning and purpose are human attributions and that events do not have an inherent purpose—unless of course the event is caused by intentional human action (or the purposeful behavior of some other animal). The belief that life is random is unsettling, but it can be emotionally liberating. Accepting randomness frees people from excessive self-blame, and in so doing also empowers them.

The Universe Has No Purpose, but We Do

The universe has no purpose, but we do. We give value and meaning to life. People can and do care, even if the universe doesn't. Once we come to terms with the universe's indifference, we realize more acutely that we have only each other to rely on. There is much we can do to alleviate each other's suffering when adversity strikes. Our support and empathy toward our fellow human beings in their time of need help them not only materially but also demonstrate to them that they matter and that what happens to them has an emotional impact on us. When we act kindly, it also gives meaning to our own lives, as we see that we matter to others. To see life dualistically divided between fair and unfair does us no favors. It's a short jump away from viewing life as a series of good and bad, should and shouldn't, and so on. However, life appears in this manner solely from our extremely narrow perspective. If we want to address the issue of fairness, we ought to be honest with ourselves about our current belief systems of what's fair and what's unfair. If we view death as being unfair, as most of us do deep in our bones, it will follow that anything resembling or reminding us of death will also register as unfair. Everything in life is continuously changing, which means we are bound to come across something we don't like at some point.

ॐ

References

1. Ralph Lewis (2019). Why Do Bad Things Happen to Good People? https://www.psychologytoday.com/intl/blog/finding-purpose/201910/why-do-bad-things-happen-to-good-people
2. Ralph Lewis (2018). Finding Purpose in a Godless World: Why We Care Even If the Universe Doesn't. Amherst, NY: Prometheus Books.
3. Rabbi Harold Kushner (1981). When Bad Things Happen to Good People. New York: Schocken Books.

XXII

The Psychology a of Happiness

Understanding Happiness

Is happiness something that can be quantified?What exactly is happiness? Happiness involves more than just feeling a positive mood. It can be considered an emotional state that indicates a significant level of mental and/or emotional wellness. Aristippus, a Greek philosopher of the 4th century BC, asserted that happiness consists of life's 'hedonic' experiences. Hedonic enjoyment refers to a condition in which a person experiences relaxation, feels a sense of detachment from their issues, and may be described as feeling 'happy' (Ryan & Deci, 2001). From the era of Aristotle, happiness has been understood to consist of at least two components – hedonic (or pleasure) and eudaimonia (the feeling that life is fulfilling) (Kringelbach & Berridge, 2010). Physical pleasures such as food, wine, and sex can undoubtedly be gratifying, and certain academics still regard them as essential to happiness. Mill argues that physical pleasures are suitable for animals, yet humans pursue higher forms of fulfillment. Cash is great! Aristotle viewed it as a "true good" similar to nourishment, rest, and companionship. However, many of us realize, at a fundamental level, that riches do not ensure joy. Money can address certain issues, but in what way can it ease the sorrow of losing a loved one, a broken marriage, or a terminal disease? There is significant evidence that the connection between wealth and happiness is quite weak.

The Science of Happiness is gaining momentum, with researchers worldwide investigating the neuroscience of happiness alongside the psychology of well-being. Human well-being consists of both hedonic and eudaimonic principles, with extensive literature that explores our meaning and purpose in life. Happiness is a condition of emotional fulfillment that can be felt in the present or regarded as an overall assessment of one's life. It is also referred to as subjective well-being (SWB). Subjective well-being (SWB) is a concept commonly utilized in psychological studies, describing how individuals assess and judge their own existence. Instead of being just one notion, SWB includes thoughtful cognitive evaluations about life satisfaction along with positive and enjoyable feelings. Research indicates that SWB is linked to improved health, increased lifespan, creativity, and enhanced job performance (Diener et al., 2018). Multiple elements affect happiness, particularly genetics, situations, and mindset. It acknowledges the significance of our mindset, attitudes, and emotions in fostering a positive relationship with ourselves, our surroundings, and others.

Theory and Science of Happiness

The construct of happiness is still evolving, and although challenging to define, it is a construct that can be empirically evaluated through qualitative and quantitative assessment. Delle Fave and colleagues (2011) noted that happiness is also an ambiguous term that can have several meanings:

- A transient emotion (that is synonymous with joy)

- An experience of fulfillment and accomplishment (characterized by a cognitive evaluation)
- A long-term process of meaning-making and identity development through achieving one's potential and the pursuit of subjectively relevant goals.

Historically, dating back to the era of Aristotle, happiness has been understood as consisting of at least two elements – hedonic (or pleasure) and eudaimonia (a feeling that life is fulfilling). As we progress into the contemporary age, there is a consensus on the elements that constitute theories of happiness. Haybron (2003) suggests that there are 3 fundamental perspectives on happiness when examining theories of the subject.

- **Hedonism** – in other words, to be happy is to experience, overall, most of the pleasure. Hedonic.
- **Life-satisfaction view** – to be happy is to have a favorable attitude about one's life, either over its entirety or just over a limited time. Eudaimonia.
- **Affective state theory** – that happiness depends on an individual's overall emotional state.

Need and Goal Satisfaction Theories: These theories propose that happiness comes from working towards suitable goals and fulfilling one's essential human needs. Deci and Ryan (2000), for instance, introduced the Self-determination Theory, which asserts that well-being is attained when individuals fulfill their fundamental human needs such as autonomy, competence, and relatedness.

Genetic and Personality Predisposition Theories: These propose that well-being is influenced by genes and is associated with the personality traits of extraversion and neuroticism. This, in turn, implies that well-being does not change much over time.

Process/Activity Theories: Process/activity theories argue that well-being may be improved by participating in activities that are engaging and require effort. This perspective suggests that happiness is relatively stable over time, and therefore efforts to increase happiness are futile (Norrish & Vella-Brodrick, 2008).

The degree of happiness a person feels relies on a combination of cognitive and emotional assessments of their life and is influenced by several factors that can be broadly categorized into three main groups: genetic and biological baseline, life situations, and deliberate actions. While personality traits like neuroticism and extraversion are thought to be rather constant (Costa & McCrae, 1980), it is still not fully understood to what extent these supposedly stable traits are entirely biologically fixed and resistant to change. View optimism as a prime illustration of this ambiguity. Although optimism seems strongly linked to the depression aspect of the personality trait of neuroticism (showing a negative correlation), it is also viewed as a cognitive explanatory style that can be acquired (Seligman, 1990).

Some Ways to Be Happier

To be happier, you can: practice gratitude, cultivate positive relationships, engage in regular physical activity, prioritize self-care, pursue hobbies, set realistic goals, spend time in nature, focus on the present moment, limit comparisons to others, and actively seek out positive experiences in your daily life. We can be happier if we embrace life's difficulties and focus more on relationships and meaning.

- Practice gratitude to increase both happiness and life satisfaction
- Forgiveness - When you can let go of anger, you may begin learning how to be happy with yourself.
- Mindfulness - Focusing on bad things and negative emotions can be destructive. You can learn to be happier when you stop dwelling on the negative and focus on the more positive side of things.

- Avoid news overdose - Unfortunately, the news too frequently is filled with stories of suffering. These stories can skew your view of the world and cause you to focus on your worst fears instead of recognizing the good that surrounds you.
- Do something meaningful each day - Putting effort into the things that matter most to you will help you use and reserve your energy in ways that will bring out the best in you.
- Purpose: A feeling of purpose and guidance, rooted in our principles and our capacity to aid the broader community. They claim that without a purpose, it's simple to stray off course when confronted with challenges. Being motivated by a sense of purpose is crucial for feeling fulfilled in life.
- Transcendence: Transcendence is the sensation of belonging to and being linked with something larger than ourselves. Whether we discover it via faith, mindfulness, or moments of wonder, it's crucial for us to occasionally step beyond our daily worries and concentrate on the broader significance of existence. Transcendence or awe can provide us with a sense of meaning and purpose, shielding us from depression and enhancing our overall well-being.
- Limit social comparison: Avoid comparing your life to others on social media.
- Positive self-talk: Challenge negative thoughts and replace them with encouraging affirmations.

There is an alternative method in which the past can assist you in the present. Studies indicate that connecting with our heritage can provide significant psychological advantages. Family narratives about triumphing over challenges, for instance, can be uplifting when transmitted to the younger generation. It can also provide you with a validating sense of perspective and appreciation—recognizing that your current life is a result of the challenges and strength exhibited by those before you for the benefit of future generations.

"The key to progress isn't perfection, it's to begin again, and again, and again. Every day is a new day, and another opportunity to pick up the hammer and go back to work," they write. "Just remind yourself that the life you want is built on love and start again."

References

1. Diener, E. (2000). Subjective well-being: The science of happiness and a proposal for a national index. American Psychologist, 55(1), 34-43.
2. Diener, E. (2025). Happiness: the science of subjective well-being. In R. Biswas-Diener & E. Diener (Eds), Noba textbook series: Psychology. Champaign, IL: DEF publishers. Retrieved from http://noba.to/qnw7g32t
3. Lyubomirsky, S. (2013). The myths of happiness: What should make you happy, but doesn't, what shouldn't make you happy, but does. New York, NY: Penguin.

XXIII

Sex Education in Schools

Sex education in schools is essential as it assists youth in acquiring the knowledge and abilities necessary for making healthy decisions. Sex education in schools is a curriculum that offers knowledge about sexuality, sexual wellness, and interpersonal relationships. It aims to assist young individuals in acquiring the knowledge and abilities required to make well-informed choices regarding their sexual health. A major issue with abstinence-only education is that it prevents teenagers from exploring acceptable alternatives besides abstinence. No type of sex education has proven to effectively discourage teenagers from engaging in sexual activity. Caregivers, teachers, and other important adults in a young person's life should encourage them and enhance their health and wellness. This should occur even if a young individual does not adhere to specific behavioral standards, whether related to sexuality or another aspect. In the last two decades, many studies have repeatedly demonstrated that providing comprehensive sex education in schools does not lead to children initiating sexual activity earlier or engaging in it more frequently. Additional research has indicated that supplying condoms in schools does not increase promiscuity among students.

"Having external condoms available does seem to encourage teens to use them, but only if they would be having sex anyway."

Comprehensive Sexuality Education or CSE

Comprehensive sexuality education, or various alternate terms, refers to a curriculum-focused approach to instructing and learning regarding the cognitive, emotional, physical, and social dimensions of sexuality. Its goal is to provide children and young individuals with the knowledge, skills, attitudes, and values that enable them to achieve their health, well-being, and dignity; foster respectful social and sexual relationships; reflect on how their decisions impact their well-being and that of others; and comprehend and safeguard their rights throughout their lives. CSE approaches sexuality positively, highlighting values like respect, inclusion, equality, non-discrimination, empathy, responsibility, and reciprocity. It strengthens beneficial and affirmative values regarding bodies, puberty, relationships, sex, and family life.

Does Sex Education Work?

Sex education provides youth with the understanding and abilities necessary for a lifetime of healthy sexual well-being. They discover how to cultivate healthy relationships, make educated choices regarding sex, analyze the world critically, support marginalized individuals, and embrace themselves for their true selves. Studies indicate that sex education that is inclusive and culturally aware aids young individuals in building the social and emotional abilities essential for becoming compassionate and empathetic adults. This form of sex education provided frequently and at an early age, fosters an understanding of sexual diversity, aids in preventing dating and intimate partner violence, promotes healthy relationship development, helps to prevent child sexual abuse, enhances social and emotional learning, and boosts media literacy.

It also assists young individuals in preventing unintended pregnancies and sexually transmitted infections (STIs). Sex education works best when it's:

- Taught by trained professionals
- Taught early and often throughout the lifespan
- Includes both information and skill-building activities
- Evidence-informed
- Inclusive of LGBTQ+ youth
- Rooted in anti-racism practices
- Trauma-informed
- Adapted to the needs of the community

The Evidence on The Impact of Sex Education:

- Sexuality education has beneficial effects, such as enhancing young people's understanding and fostering their attitudes concerning sexual and reproductive health and behaviors.

- Sexuality education encourages students to postpone their initial sexual experience, enhances their use of condoms and other contraceptives during sexual activity, boosts their understanding of their bodies and healthy relationships, reduces their tendency to take risks, and lowers the incidence of unprotected sex.
- Programs that advocate for abstinence as the sole option have proven ineffective in postponing sexual initiation, decreasing sexual activity frequency, or lowering the number of sexual partners. For effective change and to decrease early or unintended pregnancies, education on sexuality, reproductive health, and contraception needs to be comprehensive.
- Sex Education/CSE is five times more likely to be successful in preventing unintended pregnancy and sexually transmitted

infections when it pays explicit attention to the topics of gender and power

- Parents and family members are a primary source of information, values formation, care, and support for children. Sexuality education has the most impact when school-based programmes are complemented with the involvement of parents and teachers, training institutes, and youth-friendly services.

Sex education aims to provide young individuals with the knowledge and abilities required to make informed choices regarding sex and relationships throughout their lives. Studies have consistently demonstrated that teenagers gain advantages from thorough, inclusive sexual education provided in educational institutions. Sex education doesn't lead children to become more sexually active, but it raises the chances of practicing safer sex. Caregivers play a crucial role in encouraging healthy sexual attitudes and behaviors among young individuals, whether at home or in educational settings. Numerous individuals contribute to educating youth about their sexuality and sexual and reproductive health, whether through formal education, at home, or in other informal environments. Ideally, comprehensive and reliable education on these subjects should be offered from various sources. This involves parents and relatives as well as educators, who can assist in guaranteeing that young individuals receive scientific and accurate information while helping them develop critical skills. Moreover, sex education can be offered beyond the school setting, for instance, by qualified social workers and counselors who support young individuals.

"Because all youth need quality, inclusive and caring sexual healthcare, sex and relationships education and other related services, marginalized youth most of all."

— Scarleteen

References

1. Hall KS, McDermott Sales J, Komro KA, Santelli J. The state of sex education in the United States. J Adolesc Health. 2016;58(6):595-597. doi:10.1016/j.jadohealth.2016.03.032
2. Goldfarb ES, Lieberman LD. Three decades of research: the case for comprehensive sex education. Journal of Adolescent Health. 2021;68(1):13-27. doi:10.1016/j.jadohealth.2020.07.036
3. Wang T, Lurie M, Govindasamy D, Mathews C. The effects of school-based Condom Availability Programs (CAPs) on condom acquisition, use and sexual behavior: a systematic review. AIDS Behav. 2018;22(1):308-320. doi:10.1007/s10461-017-1787-5

XXIV

The Indian Education System

"Education should develop the mind, body, and character of the learner in a holistic manner".

Mahatma Gandhi

Education is essential in the lives of all individuals. Improved education empowers you to transform your life, alters your mindset entirely, and fosters confidence that aids in shaping your personality. It aids your learning, boosts your knowledge, and improves your skills. The Indian Education System must overcome several challenges and barriers to provide improved education to children, who represent the nation's future. Over the years, the Indian education system has experienced several changes; yet there are still numerous unresolved loopholes and problems. Education prepares individuals for life by equipping them with the tools to confidently confront challenges in various aspects - physically, intellectually, emotionally, and spiritually while broadening their perspective and enabling them to make wise decisions. The primary objective of education is to steer individuals toward leading a meaningful and productive life. A significant problem in education today is the unequal educational standards that often reflect socioeconomic status. Education is considered essential for an individual to thrive in society. Education is viewed as a crucial procedure for the development of human capital. Education contributes to various forms of development, including cognitive, intellectual, social, and personal advancement.

In the early days, Brahmin educators provided literacy skills to boys from Brahmin families in the traditional Hindu education system. Education in the Mogul era primarily served the affluent class rather than those of high-caste descent. These current tendencies towards elitism were reinforced even more under British rule. British colonialism brought the concept of a modern government, economy, and educational system. The educational system was established in the three presidencies (Bombay, Calcutta, and Madras). Colonial rule promoted an education system that prioritized perpetuating the privileges of the elite by linking career opportunities in government with academic instruction. In the early 1900s, the Indian National Congress supported the promotion of national education emphasizing the growth of technical and vocational skills. Congress initiated a boycott on state-funded schools in 1920, while also creating various 'national' schools and colleges. The boycott went unnoticed as the advantages of British education were too significant for the attempts to succeed. Local elites in the colony took advantage of the British education system to eventually drive out the colonizers.

Nehru envisioned India as a secular democracy with an economy controlled by the state. Ensuring everyone has access to education and promoting economic development were seen as crucial in uniting a nation fragmented by disparities in wealth, caste, and religion, and were key in resisting imperialism. Following independence, schools began emphasizing inclusivity and national pride, emphasizing the notion that India's varied communities could peacefully coexist within a single nation. The consequences of this Nehruvian educational approach are substantial; a notable outcome is the fostering of a pluralistic/secular perspective within the Indian society. IITs and IIMs offering subsidized quality higher education played a key role in Nehru's vision for a self-sufficient and contemporary India and are now esteemed institutions worldwide. Moreover, affirmative action measures in both education and employment have played a role in providing improved educational opportunities for social groups who have been historically disadvantaged. Certain marginalized groups still face limited access, but the advancement of a few Dalit and tribal families through school affirmative action and government aid has produced inspiring figures crucial for India's democracy.

Current Issues and Challenges in Education in India

The country's education system exhibits heterogeneity. The diverse nature of the education system is influenced by various factors such as where people live, their social status, ethnicity, rural or urban settings, and their backgrounds. Various types of colleges, universities, and educational institutions offer a wide range of programs. Educational institutions provide a variety of programs, courses, and quality education options. Some institutions provide high-quality education, while there are also institutions that engage in educational dishonesty. Political factors play a role in education, as many institutions are owned by influential political leaders. The current political leaders play a significant role in governing educational institutions. They have set up their booths for young people and promote the students' organization on a political level. The political agenda utilizes the students' energy and enthusiasm for its own goals. At times, students struggle to handle their education and may resort to protesting to meet their needs. Some students may even veer off from their educational goals to pursue a career in politics.

The new and desired trend of privatizing higher education is necessary to maintain creativity, flexibility, and excellence. The economic trend of liberalization and globalization calls for it. In India, both public and private institutions operate at the same time. Around half of the higher education in India is provided by private institutions, mostly without government support and involving expensive fees. Nevertheless, the condition is not deemed very humble. Private providers aim to reduce costs by compromising on the quality of education to increase profits. Encouraging creativity, logical and rational thinking, research, and the use of innovative techniques and methods is crucial at every educational level. These will help create an enjoyable learning experience. Some students lack enthusiasm for learning or going to classes, causing a rise in absenteeism rates. Learning research techniques is crucial for students as they are essential in higher education.

Scientific and technological advancements, innovative techniques, modernization, and industrial growth have diminished moral beliefs in today's world. In educational settings, teachers may give negative feedback on students' performance, leading to strained relationships between teachers and students. Today, everyone strives for respect and politeness; older students try to talk to teachers and staff if their needs are not being met. Peers are crucial in influencing the social, emotional, and character growth of students during this stage. Amid this unusual period of change, they gain important insights about support, dependence, and growth through their relationships with each other. Nevertheless, friends can negatively impact one's overall character. They may exhibit harmful behaviors like skipping school, stealing, and cheating academically. Some students are heavily impacted and may start adopting unhealthy habits such as smoking, drinking alcohol, using drugs, or developing other addictions. Children succumb to peer pressure to build a positive image among their group of friends. At times, they imitate and comply with their friends to avoid being rejected, ignored, or ridiculed if they opt out.

The substantial quality of higher education is also a notable issue. A significant increase in the number of higher education institutions has occurred, leading to a large proportion of the population enrolling in them. The significant increase in the number of students enrolling and expanding has created a major challenge in upholding standard regulations. The government is providing financial aid for higher education. Individuals who receive financial assistance for their college education are unconcerned about the quality since they do not bear a significant financial burden for it.

ಐ

References

- Marie Lall, Chatham House (2005). The Challenges for India's Education System. https://www.chathamhouse.org/sites/default/files/public/Research/Asia/bpindiaeducation.pdf
- R.N. Sharma, Indian Education at the Cross Road. Delhi: Shubhi, 2002. https://gtchooghly.ac.in/pdf/profile/goutam-patra/kothari%20commission.pdf
- Government of India. 'Selected Educational Statistics', Ministry of Human Resource Development, (MHRD), GOI, New Delhi. https://www.education.gov.in/sites/upload_files/mhrd/files/statistics-new/ESAG-2018.pdf

XXV

The Art of Decision-Making

What makes certain decisions superior to others? It relies on the quality and amount of information and reasoning used to make the decision. Inaccurate and/or insufficient information and reasoning result in misguided predictions of future results and thus poorly informed decisions due to misguided expectations regarding the consequences of a decision. A decision is considered high quality when the decision-maker understands the risks involved in making that decision. They are aware of the quality of their information and the biases present in their reasoning. A wise choice is one where you are aware of your ignorance. If a choice is made among alternatives without completely grasping the consequences of one option versus another, but the result is favorable, can it be deemed a good decision? No, it was simply a "lucky result." It was fortunate. Even poor choices can lead to lucky results.

Carefully crafted choices (sound decisions) are more likely to produce positive results. A poor choice is a hasty, ill-informed decision. The decision maker selects from options without fully grasping all the necessary information regarding the advantages and disadvantages of each choice, or if all alternatives have been considered. They are unaware of the quality of their information, whether it is good or bad. A well-informed (effective) decision relies on a thorough examination of the accessible data and logical reasoning. The quality of a decision reflects the extent to which the decision maker was informed when selecting from the available choices. A poor choice is one where the decision maker lacks adequate knowledge due to incorrect information, insufficient information, or flawed reasoning. Sound decisions are not reliant on chance. They are not merely the outcome of "rolling the dice"; they represent instances of calculated risk-taking.

Steps For Making Good Decisions

- Identify the decision: Recognize that you need to make a choice
- Gather information: Research the situation and ask questions
- Identify alternatives: Consider different options
- Evaluate options: Weigh the evidence and consider the consequences of each option
- Make a decision: Choose the best option
- Take action: Implement your decision
- Review your decision: Consider the results and how you could improve next time

Avoid putting pressure on yourself to be completely certain about any single choice; instead, focus on which option, both objectively and subjectively, aligns best with your values and objectives, considers the number of advantages compared to disadvantages, reflects how you imagine your feelings toward that choice in the future and incorporates feedback you've obtained from relevant sources on how to move forward. From that point, it's essential to dedicate yourself to that action, put in your full effort, and believe that you made the best choice you could. For many of us, making decisions can often be intimidating. However, that doesn't imply we cannot complete this task with more confidence and improved readiness. The goal isn't to make decision-making simple, necessarily—although these methods can indeed lead to this outcome. It aims to cultivate a stronger assurance in our selected choices, along with the act of choosing itself.

The domain of behavioral economics has shown that individuals do not consistently act rationally in their decision-making processes. Luckily, many personal and work-related decisions have either minor or no lasting negative outcomes. Nonetheless, there are times when an individual must choose something that will significantly influence their future—from whom they marry to where they reside to how they handle their work life. In such situations, it's crucial to steer clear of typical traps that may result in ineffective decision-making. These can involve conducting insufficient or excessive research, confusing opinions with facts, experiencing decision fatigue, not learning from previous mistakes, and others.

Think Outside the Box

'She did not know then that imagination is the beginning of creation. You imagine what you desire; you will what you imagine; and at last, you create what you will.'

-George Bernard Shaw

Thinking outside the box is a way of making decisions creatively and innovatively. It involves looking at problems from a different perspective and questioning assumptions. Consider your perspectives and beliefs. Ask yourself questions about your openness to change and your awareness of your biases. The following techniques will help you think outside the box.

- **Define The Problem:** Break down the problem into smaller parts to understand it better
- **Question Assumptions:** Consider alternative perspectives and possibilities

- **Generate Ideas:** Use brainstorming and mind mapping to come up with ideas
- **Evaluate Ideas:** Consider the feasibility, impact, and alignment with your goals
- **Refine And Act:** Implement the best ideas and monitor their progress

Instead of being narrow-minded, you ought to embrace fresh ideas and viewpoints. The initial step is becoming accustomed to contemplating matters that lie beyond your comfort zone. Considering unconventional ideas assists you in tackling difficult issues. It enables you to explore beyond a specific range of relevance to uncover solutions that wouldn't be found otherwise. Considering different perspectives also compels you to broaden your view. As you examine your surroundings, you start to notice looming dangers and possibilities. That strategic foresight allows you to stay in front of profit or loss trends since you can take proactive steps.

References

1. Christine Miller, et al., (2021). Outside the Box: Promoting Creative Problem-Solving from the Classroom to the Boardroom. Journal of Effective Teaching in Higher Education; 4(1). DOI: 10.36021/jethe.v4i1.204
2. Supiano, B. (2020). The Creativity Challenge. Chronicle of Higher Education Report. https://store.chronicle.com/products/the-creativity-challenge
3. Sawyer, K. (2012). Explaining creativity: The science of human innovation. Oxford University Press.

XXVI

Career Counselling

What is Career Counselling?

In psychology, career advice is a process that assists individuals in examining their career alternatives and choosing a course of study. Finding a job that fits with one's beliefs and interests is something that career counsellors may assist with. The core ideas of career exploration and self-awareness are the focus of career counselling. Self-concept, professional aspirations, exploring the many job possibilities and opportunities available, and making career decisions based on abilities and qualifications are the main topics of career counselling. Career counselling also entails creating both short- and long-term career plans by establishing goals and deadlines for improving one's education and skills and assisting with times of professional transition, such as changing careers, returning to the workforce after a gap, being unemployed, or retiring. Four core elements are typical characteristics of most forms of career guidance and counseling:

1. A focus on psychologically healthy clients.
2. A focus on the client's resources and strengths.

3. A relatively short duration of the guidance/counseling process; and

4. Considering the client in context (Gelso & Fretz, 2001).

Importance of Career

Most individuals work for financial benefit, but for some, employment is a method of establishing identity. It also offers kids a sense of value and promotes self-image. A person's profession affects his or her whole life, both physically and mentally. The individual's whole lifestyle is influenced by their profession choice. According to Imbimbo (1994), "There are interconnections between work roles and other life roles". So, we may conclude that an individual's profession choice influences his or her income, social identity, social position, economic status, purpose of life, friends, education, and even the clothing they wear! Career growth may assist an individual find more fulfillment in his life because a career is an essential component of life. Research has shown that people who actively manage their careers generally:

- Higher sense of meaningfulness in their lives.
- Have high levels of life satisfaction and success in personal goals.
- Are well-informed, who can learn, unlearn, and re-learn
- Could make job and education choices that
- Experience less stress and therefore have fewer physical and emotional problems.
- Can cope with life changes such as moving between jobs, becoming a student, becoming unemployed, or retiring
- Are open to new possibilities and experiences to help them succeed in their goals.

According to studies, young people who graduate from school without a clear career path are more likely to experience long-term disadvantages such as higher unemployment rates, part-time and casual employment, shorter working lives, lower incomes, and a higher likelihood of landing in positions with worse working conditions and fewer opportunities for advancement. Along with greater crime rates and worse physical and mental health, they are also less likely to engage in activities that might help them contribute to society.

Importance of Career Counselling

The process of selecting a career is unique to everyone. Several factors influence the choice of a career. Some of the important factors that have a role to play are personality factors, aptitude and interest of the individual, developmental stage of the person; his/her value system, and life roles. Age and gender also influence career choices. It is unfortunate that despite the recognition of the importance of career counselling, it does not enjoy the same status as counseling and psychotherapy. This form of counselling is often misunderstood and often unappreciated. This is unfortunate for both the counselling profession as well as for the persons who need it!

Crites (1981) states the important aspects of career counselling:

- "The need for career counselling is greater than the need for psychotherapy" – as career counselling deals with the inner as well as the outer world of the individual whereas all other counselling approaches only deal with the inner reality.
- "Career counselling can be therapeutic" – research has indicated a positive correlation between career and personal adjustment. Clients who learn to successfully deal with problems at the workplace can extend their skills to social as well as other problem areas.
- "Career counselling is more difficult than psychotherapy" – in continuation with the second point, it is important to understand that career counselling requires proficiency not only in being able to help the client deal with internal problems, as

in the case of counselling and psychotherapy but also have the required information to give a direction to the client's career. The care counselor is required to draw information not only from personality theories but also from the various career development theories.

According to Krumboltz (1994), career and personal counselling are inextricably intertwined and must be dealt with together if the client is to benefit from the counselling process. It cannot be denied that a person who loses a job and is unable to find something of his interest has a problem not only related to his career but is also having problems of anxiety, uncertainty, lowered self-esteem, as well as stress related to psychological, social as well as financial issues. This person, therefore, must be dealt with holistically.

The Process of Self-Discovery

One important aspect of career counselling is the assessment of different aspects of the client that will help in appropriate career choices. An awareness of the needs, aspirations, aptitude, personality type, and value system of the client helps ensure the selection of the right career as well as avoiding later frustration and attrition. Toward this end, counselors are usually involved in dealing with four distinct but sometimes overlapping categories of tests: Aptitude, interest, personality, and achievement.

- **Aptitude:** An aptitude is the capability to perform a specific type of work at a certain standard. Aptitudes can be either physical or mental. It is different from knowledge, understanding, or learned abilities (skills), as well as from attitudes. Aptitude is distinct from achievement, which reflects the knowledge or skills obtained after completing a training program. An aptitude test evaluates an individual's potential to benefit from training in a particular profession or skill. Formeasuring aptitude, aptitude tests are usually divided into two categories:

- Multi-aptitude batteries,which test many skills by administering a battery of tests,
- Component ability tests thatassess a single ability or skill such as music or mechanical ability. Some of the best-known multi-aptitudebatteries are the Scholastic Aptitude Test (SAT), and the Differential Aptitude Test (DAT) by Bennet,Seashore, and Wesman.

- **Interest:** Interest describes the attitude characterized by a need to give selective attention to something significant to a person such as an activity, goal, or research area. For measuring interest, interest inventoryis designed specifically for this purpose.There are various types of interest inventory such as Self-Directed Search (SDS) by John Holland, the KuderOccupational Interest Survey (KOIS), and Career Beliefs Inventory (CBI) by John D Krumboltz. Fornon-college students, there are interest inventories like Clark's Minnesota Vocational Interest Inventoryand Johansson's Career Assessment Inventory.
- **Personality:** The term 'Personality' pertains to the distinctive patterns of thought, emotion, and behavior that characterize an individual, along with the psychological processes – both visible and hidden – that underlie these patterns. Personality assessments are systematic methods employed to evaluate personality. A personality assessment can be a technique used to analyze personality, such as through checklists, personality assessments, and projective methods. These assessments are generally categorized into two primary types: objective and projective. A well-known objective assessment is the Myers–Briggs Type Indicator (MBTI). Projective assessments encompass the Rorschach Inkblot Test created by Hermann Rorschach and the Thematic Apperception Test (TAT) developed by Henry Murray.
- **Achievement:** Achievement is viewed basically as the competence a person has in an area of content. Achievement tests are there to measure an individual's degree of

accomplishment or learning in a subject or task. Instruments are also available that measure achievement such as the Adult Basic Learning Examination and the Tests of General Education Development (GED).

Encouraging participants to engage in the process is one of the major challenges associated with career counselling. Clients often tend to reject the interventions made by professional career counsellors preferring to rely on the advice of peers, senior family members, or superiors within their profession. A career counsellor also needs to keep in touch with the many job options – traditional as well as non-traditional. Developments around the world are impacting the field of careers as well. "The information age continues to alter the number of job openings as well as how a wide variety of jobs is done" (Walls & Fuller, 1996).

Career counselling encompasses a broad range of professional activities aimed at assisting individuals in navigating career-related obstacles—serving both as a preventive strategy and in challenging circumstances. Career counsellors support clients with all aspects related to challenges in this area. They address issues such as unemployment, as well as conflicts with colleagues, subordinates, or superiors. Guidance on achieving career success and advancing in one's profession also falls within the career counsellor's domain. Career counsellors collaborate with individuals from various backgrounds, including young people exploring career choices, seasoned professionals considering a shift in their careers, mothers seeking to return to the workforce after a break to care for their children, or older adults looking for re-employment for financial reasons or to lead a more fulfilling life. Career counselling is available in different environments, both in group settings and one-on-one sessions.

References

1. Hirschi, A., & Froidevaux, A. (2020). Career Counselling. In H. Gunz, M. Lazarova, & W. Mayrhofer, Routledge Companion to Career Studies (pp. 331-345). London, UK: Routledge. The final chapter is available, upon publication, at: https://doi.org/10.4324/9781315674704

2. Anderson, W. P., & Niles, S. G. (2000). Important events in career Counselling: Client and counsellor descriptors. Career Development Quarterly, 48, 251-263.

XXVII

The Existential Crisis

Existential crises are perplexing and anxiety-filled moments when an individual strives to understand and answer the question: Who am I? An existential crisis is a time of deep self-examination and exploration of life's purpose and your role in the universe. It may lead to sensations of bewilderment, unease, and hopelessness. An existential crisis refers to the discomfort individuals feel regarding meaning, choices, and freedom in their lives. This existential anxiety may lead you to believe that life is fundamentally meaningless and that existence lacks significance. An existential crisis may result in uncertainty regarding your sense of self. Existential anxiety often emerges during periods of change and indicates challenges in adjustment, frequently associated with a sense of losing safety and security.

Identifying an Existential Crisis

During an existential crisis, a person may experience a variety of symptoms, including:

- Anxiety
- Depression
- Feeling overwhelmed - A deep longing for meaning

- Isolation - Feelings of emptiness, alienation, or futility
- Sudden interest in philosophical or spiritual matters
- Lack of motivation and energy
- Loneliness
- Obsessive worry
- Unexplained fear
- Persistent relationship conflicts or doubts about relationships

While the specific traits of an existential crisis differ among psychologists, the majority agree that it fundamentally represents a phase of anxiety and struggle regarding the purpose and the meaning of life. Certain psychologists concentrate on the existential crisis as an inquiry into identity and the individual's desired self. Some argue that it centers on the balance between feelings of obligation and dedication versus autonomy and liberation. Many suggest it is an encounter with insights regarding existential truths like death. An existential struggle is frequently viewed as linked to spirituality since numerous individuals derive significance from spiritual activities.

Psychologists have identified unique emotional, cognitive, and behavioral elements of an existential crisis. The emotional aspect might encompass feelings like despair, helplessness, guilt, fear, anxiety, and loneliness. The cognitive aspect may encompass thoughts regarding a deficit of meaning and purpose, mortality, and uncertainty. The behavioral aspect might involve a lack of action, actions leading to relationship breakdowns, addictive habits, and pursuing various forms of therapy. An existential crisis lasts for an extended duration with unsettling emotions, making it hard to differentiate from depression; indeed, these two states can sometimes coincide. Major depression, according to the Diagnostic and Statistical Manual of Mental Disorders, 5th edition (DSM-5), encompasses similar symptoms like anxiety and hopelessness, but these symptoms persist longer and significantly impair one's ability to function in everyday life. The connection between existential crises and depression could be causal. Psychologists are especially focused on the connection between specific forms of situational depression and existential crises, as understanding this link may aid in identifying the most effective treatment.

Measuring the Degree of Having an Existential Crisis

When assessing the extent of an existential crisis, two primary areas to focus on are relationships and careers. Individuals in a dysfunctional relationship or stuck in an unfulfilling job often face an existential crisis. The severity of their existential crisis is influenced by the quality of their relationship and their level of job dissatisfaction. A relationship is deemed broken if it results in several factors. The factors ordered from most negative to least negative include murder, abuse (both physical and mental), constant fighting, and cohabiting without communication. An individual facing any of those factors with their partner will be undergoing an existential crisis to varying extents. Indicators that individuals are unhappy with their jobs include appearing disengaged, failing to create quality original work, and choosing to retire earlier than necessary.

Later Existential Crisis

In later adulthood, after having built a career, formed relationships, and faced identity-related questions, an individual may still encounter a different kind of existential crisis. The subsequent existential crisis happens later in life's second half. Individuals facing a later existential crisis might grapple with concerns related to illness, bodily suffering, and anxiety about imminent mortality, yet this late existential crisis is not solely focused on addressing those concerns. It focuses on the desire to enhance one's life before occurrences like sickness and demise take control. Particularly, the subsequent existential crisis encompasses reflections on ethics, legacy, and accomplishments. Regarding morality, people might reflect on previous misdeeds and find it challenging to discover a means to rectify them while they still have a chance. Individuals confronting the legacy and accomplishment facets of the later existential crisis seek assurance that they have positively influenced their career, family, or the world at large. They wish to create a significant legacy and accomplish everything possible before time runs out. If they do not completely address concerns from the sophomore or adult existential crisis, they will face greater challenges with the achievement aspect. Before the eventual existential crisis is settled, individuals in distress will feel anxious by ruminating on how things might have been different, or they may sink into depression believing there is no solution to the crisis before their time runs out.

How to Cope with Meaninglessness

Yalom's (1980) research indicates that when people confront issues such as Death, Freedom, Isolation, and Meaninglessness, their overall quality of life significantly declines, leading them to engage in harmful or dangerous behaviors, such as thoughts of suicide. Yalom contends that for individuals to lead a fulfilling and meaningful life, they need to liberate themselves from these existential worries, typically via acceptance, community, and authenticity. It has been contended, however, that the main cause or factor of an existential crisis is specifically a deficiency of meaning and purpose in life (Yalom, 1980). A deficiency of meaning can stem from various sources; therefore, it is essential to pinpoint where the breach of meaning has taken place. Here, we emphasize several areas where meaning could be diminished:

1. Personal injury or personal ill health
2. Difficulties with work or finances
3. Breakdown of important relationships (e.g., a divorce or loss of a loved one)
4. Violation of basic needs (i.e., shelter, access to health care, food, and sanitation)
5. Concern over societal issues and the state of the world (i.e., political, economic, environmental, and humanitarian issues)

Experiencing a sense that life is devoid of meaning or purpose can be daunting and confusing, overshadowing everyday life. This deep feeling of meaninglessness frequently appears as a widespread void, where previously defined goals and aspirations appear to fade into a haze of doubt. The experience can cause individuals to feel lost as if they are journeying through life without a guide or direction. The emotional burden of this separation can create a deep feeling of loneliness, hindering the ability to experience happiness or fulfillment in daily tasks. To address feelings of meaninglessness, you might consider practices such as: fostering gratitude, intentionally looking for meaningful activities and relationships, examining personal values, practicing mindfulness, writing in a journal about your thoughts and feelings, and seeking professional help if necessary; ultimately, striving to discover purpose and significance by concentrating on what matters to you and actively participating in the world around you.

- Rediscover what truly holds significance for you. Consider your core values, passions, and interests. Participating in endeavors that align with these beliefs can aid in restoring a feeling of purpose and fulfillment.
- Surround yourself with supportive friends, family members, or community groups. Expressing your feelings to others can enhance your mood and provide fresh perspectives.
- Engage in mindfulness techniques to remain grounded and alleviate worries about what lies ahead. Meditation can assist you in cultivating an accepting awareness of your thoughts and feelings, offering clarity and diminishing the effects of adverse thinking patterns.
- If feelings of meaninglessness persist or become overwhelming, consider reaching out to a mental health expert for assistance. Therapy provides a secure environment to examine core problems, obtain understanding, and cultivate coping techniques.

- Prioritize activities that promote well-being and mental health (maintaining a healthy lifestyle with regular exercise, balanced nutrition, and adequate rest). Self-care practices can elevate your mood, increase energy levels, and strengthen overall resilience.
- Expressing yourself through creative outlets such as writing, art, or music can be therapeutic. Engaging in creative tasks can foster a feeling of achievement and enable you to express and examine your feelings positively.
- Spending time in nature can produce a soothing and stabilizing influence. The beauty and tranquility of nature can redirect attention from personal conflicts and offer a fresh perspective and gratitude for life.

Dealing with feelings of meaninglessness is a highly individual process that requires recognizing and tackling both the internal and external influences that lead to these sentiments. Participating in self-reflection, establishing goals, seeking assistance, and integrating self-care routines are essential actions in managing these difficult emotions. Online counseling is especially advantageous, providing flexible access to professional assistance no matter where you are. In India, leading psychologists focus on assisting people in discovering meaning and purpose in their lives. By engaging with these specialists, people can obtain customized advice and assistance designed to fit their specific situations. Keep in mind that the quest for meaning is a continual journey, and with determination and patience, it is achievable to regain a feeling of purpose and happiness.

References

1. Weems CF, et al. (2016). Existential anxiety among adolescents exposed to disaster: Linkages among level of exposure, PTSD,

and depression symptoms. J Trauma Stress; 29(5):466-473. doi:10.1002/jts.22128

2. Mary Andrews (2016). The Existential Crisis. Behavioral Development 21(1):104-109. DOI: 10.1037/bdb0000014

3. Steger, Michael F. (2020). Man's Search for Meaning: The New Theory of Happiness. Oxford University Press.

XXVIII

Understanding LGBTQ+

The term LGBTQ (which includes LGBTQAP+, LGBTQA, GLBTIQ, LGBT, and other variations) is a broad designation that represents lesbian, gay, bisexual, transgender, intersex, and queer or questioning individuals. Identifying as LGBTIQ+ does not guarantee that a person will face mental health challenges, but it may indicate a greater likelihood of encountering mental health difficulties. Issues related to mental health, including depression, self-injury, substance abuse, and suicidal ideation, can impact anyone, yet they are more prevalent among those who identify as LGBTIQ+. Identifying as LGBTIQ+ is not the reason for these issues. However, certain challenges faced by LGBTIQ+ individuals can impact their mental well-being, including discrimination, homophobia or transphobia, feelings of social isolation, rejection, and challenging experiences related to coming out. It is crucial to recognize that accepting one's LGBTIQ+ identity can positively affect an individual's well-being as well. This could indicate increased confidence, a feeling of belonging to a community, sensations of relief and self-acceptance, and improved relationships with friends and family.

Understanding LGBTQ+ Communities

On September 6, 2018, India legalized same-sex relationships, representing a significant milestone in acknowledging LGBTQ rights in the nation. India's inaugural Pride March took place in Kolkata in March 1999. However, accurate systematically gathered information on the prevalence of LGBTQ+ individuals in India is lacking since the 2011 Census did not effectively document this data.[6] In India, many Hijra, Kothis, and Transgender individuals (HKT) resort to traditional income methods (logon, cholla, and badhai) because of inadequate education and job prospects, adversely affecting their mental, physical, and sexual well-being. The HKT members who depend on cholla (begging in streets and on trains) and logon (performing at weddings through singing and dancing) face a higher risk of sexual abuse and survival sex (officially referred to as prostitution or sex work). Men who engage in sexual activity with men (MSMs) experience depression linked to discrimination stemming from their sexual orientation, gender identity, experiences of physical or sexual violence, alcohol consumption, sexually transmitted infections (STI), and HIV status. A study indicated a prevalence rate of 52.9% for psychiatric disorders among MSMs based on the General Health Questionnaire (GHQ), which assesses somatic symptoms, anxiety and insomnia, social dysfunction, and major depression.

Youth from the LGBTQ community are at a higher risk of being bullied. Victims of bullying in schools who identify as LGBTQ experience increased absenteeism and decreased academic performance. It has been associated with emotional turmoil, physical issues like anxiety and headaches, sensations of isolation and self-criticism, along with depression, and worry. Households that adhere to heteronormative beliefs contribute to the distress experienced by LGBTQ youth. Homeless LGBTQ youth experience heteronormative beliefs, stigma, and discrimination at home, resulting in serious physical and mental health issues, such as participation in risky sexual activities, substance use, and family disputes arising from the revelation of their sexual orientation. Numerous LGBTQ youth become homeless after revealing their identity to their parents and experiencing rejection. Research indicates that 37% of individuals contacting crisis service providers face homelessness, with a significant portion of those in foster care or unstable housing identifying as LGBTQ youth. LGBTQ youth encounter mental health problems such as depression, anxiety, suicidal thoughts, and substance misuse, resulting in varied performance in school.

Addressing LGBTQ+ Mental Health

Today's LGBTQ youth mature during a period of significant social and political shifts concerning LGBTQ rights and visibility while still facing risks to their mental health. Even with improvements in personal treatment approaches, school-focused initiatives, and governmental policies that tackle LGBTQ mental health, a significant void still exists in extensive evidence-based prevention and intervention programs aimed at fostering the healthy development and mental well-being of LGBTQ youth. LGBTQ+ young individuals face health inequalities when compared to heterosexual and cisgender young people. Community-centered, positive youth development organizations serve as a crucial resource to support and validate LGBTQ+ youth. In comparison to adults, considerably less research has been conducted on adolescents, with very few studies including longitudinal follow-up exceeding one year. Given the historical evolution of social acceptance for the LGBTQ+ community, fresh groups are necessary to depict current life experiences and related health outcomes. Innovative methodologies are required for sampling LGBTQ+ populations. There has been a limited amount of intervention research, and methods should consider natural resiliencies, life-course frameworks, prevention science, various levels of influence, and the significance of implementation. Regulatory hurdles arise when ethics committees choose to mandate parental consent, necessitating ethical research.

There is a significant necessity for additional health research focused on LGBTQ+ youth. As we transition into a period of evidence-based healthcare where validation of an intervention's efficacy is increasingly necessary for funding, LGBTQ+ youth frequently get overlooked due to insufficient research to show program effectiveness for this demographic. Utilizing a program found in the compendium is frequently necessary to obtain funding for HIV prevention, with comparable criteria in place for other health concerns. In the absence of foundational research guiding intervention creation and clinical trials proving efficacy, LGBTQ+ individuals frequently find themselves lacking effective solutions for their health requirements. Research on the effective provision of services should also focus on dissemination and implementation. Future studies should commence with fundamental research instead of focusing on intervention research and conclude by addressing certain obstacles to achieving this work.

Studies on health outcome differences among transgender and gender nonconforming youth have not been based on population samples; however, community-based research has indicated the presence of health disparities. Future research directions should prioritize sexual minorities instead of gender minorities (e.g., transgender) and youth, as these areas of study are somewhat separate and are at significantly different stages of scientific advancement. Overall, there has been a lack of extensive research on the health of transgender and gender nonconforming young people, and the clinical studies that have taken place have primarily concentrated on outcomes associated with gender transitions. There is a need for new longitudinal cohort studies focused on LGBTQ+ youth, due to the scarcity of previous research and the fact that current ongoing cohorts may not accurately reflect the experiences of LGBTQ+ individuals who are teenagers today, considering the swift changes in social acceptance of this group. This swift shift in social acceptance poses a challenge for longitudinal cohort studies since it is hard to differentiate developmental effects from historical changes. In addition to recording disparities, studies should concentrate on understanding the mechanisms that clarify disparities or intra-group risks affecting health drivers within LGBTQ+ communities.

Mainstream society continues to view same-sex marriages negatively. The family unit or close relationships that the heterosexual community considers normal are viewed as a privilege by them. The absence of affection, validation, and acceptance exposes them to the threat of an identity crisis, sensations of rejection, and despair. To add to the problem, mental health problems are viewed as a taboo in the nation. Requesting assistance for a mental health concern isn't well-received by friends or family in this context. Consider the struggles faced by the LGBTQ community given this context. Furthermore, there is limited psychiatric literature available in India regarding LGBTQ. Despite all the conflicts, the community members flourish and exhibit resilience. What they seek is a bit of acknowledgment and affection from their families and loved ones. Humanity takes precedence over sexual orientation and the complexities that come with it.

References

1. World Health Organization (2018). Mental health: Strengthening our response, viewed 01 October 2020, from https://www.who.int/news-room/fact-sheets/detail/mental-health-strengthening-our-response

2. Takács, J, (2015). Homophobia and Genderphobia in the European Union: Policy contexts and empirical evidence, Swedish Institute for European Policy Studies, Stockholm. https://real.mtak.hu/23603/1/2015_Takacs_Homophobia-and-genderphobia-in-the-EU_Sieps.pdf

3. The Times of India (2018). Supreme court decriminalises section 377: All you need to know | India News - Times of India. Available online at: https://timesofindia.indiatimes.com/india/sc-verdict-on-section-377-all-you-need-to-know/articleshow/65695884.cms

4. UNDP. (2010). Hijras/Transgender women in India: HIV, Human rights and social exclusion. New York: UNDP.

5. Patel V., Mayer K., Makadon H. (2012). Men who have sex with men in India: A diverse population in need of medical attention. Indian J. Med. Res. 136 563–570. https://journals.lww.com/ijmr/fulltext/2012/36040/
Men_who_have_sex_with_men_in_India__A_diverse.6.aspx

Epilogue

Leading a meaningful life means focusing on what genuinely matters to you according to your values and beliefs and continuously making progress toward those priorities. Leading a purposeful life means aligning with your values and passions while seeking joy and fulfillment. Living a meaningful life entail discovering fulfillment in being true to your genuine self, creating a beneficial influence on those around you, and continually pursuing self-improvement and understanding. Possessing a sense of purpose enhances self-esteem, motivates personal and career growth, and results in increased happiness and satisfaction. It allows you to create a beneficial effect on the world and leads to a more satisfying and rewarding life experience. Uncovering your purpose cannot be done swiftly in just a few days, weeks, or months. Reaching this objective could span a lifetime, so it's crucial to concentrate on each step individually. At times, you might find that your objectives change as time progresses. It's essential to take time to evaluate if your actions align with your objectives. If that's not the case, you have the option to alter your path. Occasionally, the path to discovering your purpose may include twists, deviations, and signals.

Attaining good mental health involves tackling existing challenges while fostering happiness and wellness. Anyone can develop a mental health problem, no matter their age, gender, socioeconomic status, or ethnicity. An individual's mental health can be affected by social and economic factors, negative childhood experiences, biological impacts, and pre-existing health conditions. Roughly one out of every four individuals experience mental illness at some stage in their life, and nearly the same proportion of children is impacted. It is a frequent and manageable health issue that significantly affects the quality of life for people and their families. Numerous myths and misconceptions about mental health are prevalent. This can make it more difficult for individuals with mental health challenges to search for and receive appropriate help and intensify the stigma they face. They may also obstruct the public's understanding of mental health. Mental health encompasses our emotional, psychological, and social wellness. It influences our thoughts, emotions, and behaviors, and plays a role in how we cope with stress, connect with others, and make decisions. Mental well-being is crucial at all stages of life, from childhood and teenage years to adulthood. Positive mental health involves the ability to think, feel, and react in the necessary and desired ways for living your life. Nonetheless, in a period of compromised mental health, you might find that your typical ways of thinking, feeling, or responding become difficult, or even overwhelming, to cope with. This can be equally as troubling as a physical illness, or maybe even more.

Higher education institutions in our country are asked to undertake important roles in developing the capability for interactive cooperation and collaborative efforts to address complex challenges impacting our world. An essential element of fostering healthy communities like education is encouraging equity and inclusion. Education is a dynamic process that encompasses deliberate actions, structure, and objectives. It activates and brings forth dormant energies and imaginative urges. The primary feature of the self is that it is a phenomenon that contemplates itself. Reflexivity enables individuals to view themselves as objects, engage in self-reflection, hold internal discussions, evaluate themselves, and beyond. Contrary to what we frequently learn in our childhood, acquiring knowledge isn't just about recalling answers. It goes beyond mere education and acquiring qualifications. Learning is not measured by exams, which merely test our understanding of theories, but is judged by its practical significance through real-world experience. Individual learning primarily centers on personal growth and development. It enhances self-confidence, problem-solving abilities, efficiency, performance, and overall experience application. Anticipation goes beyond predicting and choosing positive trends while avoiding negative ones. It also creates new alternatives. Studying differs from reading; it is challenging. Staying focused during study sessions is a difficulty encountered by both seasoned Ph.D. candidates and novice high school freshmen. To focus on academic activities, you might have to adjust your study habits, choose a calm environment without distractions, explore different methods, or establish a structured study schedule with regular mental breaks. Focus on enhancing your understanding of a topic rather than merely repeating another person's thoughts to make the learning experience more enjoyable and captivating. It is also crucial to include retrieval practice in your study routine. Ultimately, ensure you get ample sleep, maintain your hydration, and give yourself a break.

Indian parents often mistakenly believe that sports hinder their children's academic success, leading them to prevent their kids from participating in sports throughout their school and college years. Nevertheless, sports are an endeavor that produces notable benefits for people of every age group. Engaging in sports such as boxing, swimming, and various physical activities enhances brain function related to memory and cognition, leading to improved performance in academics as well. Along with the benefits to an individual's physical and mental health, sports play a crucial role in effectively combating drug and substance abuse. Addiction is a persistent but controllable health problem. Healing takes time, drive, and assistance, yet by dedicating yourself to transformation, you can conquer your addiction and take back charge of your life. The first step in addressing substance use disorder is handling withdrawal. This is the moment when you stop using the substance, allowing it to leave your system. Depending on the severity, a healthcare provider may recommend medication to lessen the effects of withdrawal symptoms, which can be difficult both physically and mentally.

The fight-or-flight response is an immediate reaction to danger that triggers physical alterations in the body's nervous system and hormonal levels, gearing up a person or animal to confront the threat or escape from it. In the fight-or-flight response, your body focuses on prioritizing tasks, putting on hold anything that isn't essential for immediate survival. The fight-or-flight response ought to be activated only when it is necessary or advantageous. The sympathetic nervous system triggers the body's reactions, whereas the parasympathetic nervous system brings the body back to a peaceful state. Managing your stress reaction is crucial for your overall health. Mental and emotional issues such as depression and bipolar disorder are often linked to suicidal ideation. At this time, feeling hopeless about the future may cause you to mistakenly think that suicide is a solution. An individual undergoes trauma when they perceive a particular situation or several situations as threatening or hazardous to their life. There are no established guidelines regarding which experiences are deemed traumatic. It all relies on how you respond to them. The most difficult aspect is that trauma related to work is often disregarded. Work-related trauma affects more than just the professional lives of employees. This invasion of their private lives can lead to a range of adverse outcomes: stressing their relationships, lowering their self-worth, obstructing their interests, and ultimately diminishing their overall health.

Recognizing when we conform offers numerous practical benefits in everyday life, depending on your objectives: it can help in understanding your behaviors and anticipating how others may respond in different scenarios. Indeed, the conformity bias may cause people to unthinkingly imitate the group rather than trust their moral judgment. People might adhere to social standards to avoid facing punishment, ridicule, or social exclusion for not fitting in with others. They may also modify their actions to receive acceptance or affection from other members of the group. Inactive employees favor a simpler approach. Simultaneously, introverts thrive when guiding proactive team members who offer numerous ideas for improvements. Introverts can assess, analyze, evaluate, and make thoughtful choices. Introverts can only become exceptional leaders by embracing their true strengths and confidently supporting their choices.

Many young individuals lack the environments, activities, and milestones that offer structure in their lives. Encouraging them to set objectives can create a structure that aids in sustaining their drive and focus on what's ahead. Setting goals can help young people focus on their ambitions, stay motivated, and boost their confidence. Goals give us a target to strive for, a motivation to keep us inspired, and, with a bit of luck and significant effort – something to celebrate. Mindfulness is an exceptional practice of reclaiming and mastering one's wholeness, which has been associated with comprehensive theoretical and empirical research showing its impact on mental wellness. Mindfulness-based approaches seek to improve mindfulness by fostering awareness of present experiences from a standpoint of calmness and acceptance. Mindfulness is a cognitive trait, a state of promoting awareness through mindfulness meditation and mental activities. Participating in mindfulness practices can aid in reorganizing your brain, redirect your attention away from negative and distracting thoughts, and enable you to connect with your surroundings while providing greater clarity to your thoughts.

The dependence on social media is a modern phenomenon, yet it has progressively become more widespread in recent times. A recent study indicates that a psychologist predicts approximately 10% of people will meet the criteria for a type of social media addiction. We need a plan to support children in both online and offline contexts that considers each child's circumstances while aiming to improve the safety and well-being of their digital environments. The effect of stress on the development and progression of depression can be seen because of multiple interrelated factors, including the continuous effects of environmental stress and the lasting repercussions of stressful experiences during childhood, both of which may contribute to prolonged hyperactivity of the hypothalamic-pituitary-adrenal axis. The effects of chronic or long-term stress can be harmful on their own; however, they may also result in depression, a mood disorder characterized by feelings of sadness and a disinterest in activities you usually enjoy. Depression can affect your eating habits, sleeping patterns, and ability to concentrate. Motivation signifies the urge to undertake actions in pursuit of a goal. Thus, it is essential to set and achieve our goals. It's a vital human necessity that supports our survival and interaction with the world. Exploring and applying motivational science can help us tackle or regulate impulsive urges, habitual actions, goal failures, inadequate performance, adverse emotions, boredom, destructive or unproductive development, and a fragile self-image.

It's important to remember that psychoanalysis seeks to reveal deeper insights into a person's mind, which is quite different from our present view on the practice and use of psychoanalysis and psychotherapy. Especially for practitioners in the area who engage in the practical process, the ideas of id, ego, and superego deconstruction along with dream interpretation signify overly simplistic techniques and ideas that are improbable to adequately address the issues contemporary mental health services seek to solve. The tribal mentality observed in people is a significant characteristic for evolution, yet the increasing tribal splits pose a serious risk to our individualistic society. Identifying people from various tribes offered evolutionary benefits for safety. Minor, unreasonable differences can effortlessly trick our minds into including or ignoring something. The brain plays a vital role in shaping cognitive, emotional, and social skills. A captivating trait of the brain is its inherent tendency towards social bonds. Human beings naturally thrive in social settings and seek out relationships with each other.

Forgiveness can improve relationships, reduce stress and anger, and increase happiness and hopefulness. If you find it difficult to initiate the process, acknowledge and communicate the elements you want to forgive. Forgiveness doesn't mean erasing the past or ignoring what happened. It doesn't guarantee that the other person will change their actions - you cannot affect that. It just means you are letting go of the anger and pain and moving toward a better circumstance. Demonstrating behaviors regarded as exceptionally "bad" can stem from multiple influences, including a lack of self-awareness. Nonetheless, this does not consistently define an individual's identity. The essence of humanity is defined by imperfections. Every individual faces challenges, makes mistakes, displays poor decisions, or says things they later regret. These instances don't label you as a "bad" person; they merely show your humanity. The classification of individuals as "good" or "bad" usually comes from how others view your recurring actions and character qualities. If you typically act with compassion, understanding, and fairness, for example, you may be regarded as "good." Being "good," however, doesn't mean that an individual cannot or will not commit wrongful acts. By understanding the motives behind why good people engage in misconduct, you're fostering your traits of kindness, including empathy and compassion.